The
LINEN HOUSES
of the
LAGAN VALLEY

The river Lagan

Herbert R. Lilley

From a Private Collection

The
LINEN HOUSES
of the
LAGAN VALLEY

The story of their families

KATHLEEN RANKIN

ULSTER HISTORICAL
FOUNDATION

Dedicated

to

Living Linen

which has done so much to ensure that
Irish linen heritage is not forgotten

Published 2002
by the Ulster Historical Foundation
12 College Square East, Belfast, BT1 6DD
www.ancestryireland.com

Printed by ColourBooks Ltd
Design and production, Dunbar Design

ISBN 1-903688-20-5

CONTENTS

4
LAMBEG

5
DRUMBEG

6
DUNMURRY

7
FINAGHY

8
EDENDERRY

ACKNOWLEDGEMENTS

A book of this nature requires an input of knowledge from a considerable number of sources.

I would like to take this opportunity to thank the many people who have helped to make this work possible, in particular the members of a small committee, John R. Cowdy, Robert J. McKinstry, Peter J. Rankin, Trevor A.R. Neill and J. Fred Rankin who gave helpful knowledge and advice. I am deeply indebted to the owners of the many houses who have allowed photographs to be taken and also, in some cases, provided family photographs. They often contributed information concerning the history of their houses and this has been of great assistance. My thanks are also due to Brian Mackey, Curator of the Irish Linen Centre and Lisburn Museum, who provided helpful advice, and many photographs of houses and portraits of their owners. In particular, I would also like to thank both Bill Crawford and Peter Rankin who read the script and made suggestions for which I am very grateful.

Where possible modern photographs of the houses have been used and, on occasion, an older photograph included for comparison. Unfortunately a considerable number of the 'Linen Houses' no longer exist and photographs have had to be sourced from former owners or local museums and libraries. This book endeavours, wherever possible, to give some idea of the lifestyle of the people who lived in the 'Linen Houses'. Many of their descendants are still alive and my thanks are due in very great measure to them for photographs of houses and their residents. I am grateful to the following for photographs: Michael Harnett, Donald Liddell, John Turner, Brian Snodden, Peter Rankin, Patrick Corkey, John Press, Rosie Castagner, Elise Coburn, Moyne Ramsey, Rachel Torrens-Spence, Susan Cunningham, Dorothy Cowdy, Robin Reade, Vera Morrison, Robin Charley, Finlay McCance, Fiona Haldane, Eileen Black, Frances Weir, Maureen King, John Adgey, Hugh Montgomery and Rev. C.W. Bell.

Acknowledgement must also be made to the various institutions that assisted with archive material and photographic research, and that have kindly given permission for photographs to be reproduced from their collections: the Public Record Office of Northern Ireland (PRONI), the Historic Monuments and Buildings Branch of the Department of the Environment for Northern Ireland (HMBB), the National Library of Ireland (NLI), the Trustees of the National Museums and Galleries of Northern Ireland: Ulster Museum (UM) and Ulster Folk and Transport Museum (UFTM), Irish Linen Centre & Lisburn Museum (ILC & LM), Lisburn Historical Society, *Belfast Telegraph*, Rathmore Grammar School, the Trustees of the Delacherois Estate, the Controller of Her Majesty's Stationery Office on behalf of the Ordnance Survey of Northern Ireland.

Lastly, I owe a very great debt to my husband, Fred, who entered into the project with great enthusiasm, and is responsible for the majority of the photographs in this book. With the inclusion of many illustrations it became clear that sponsorship support was required from outside bodies. I am extremely grateful to those listed for their generous contributions:

The Miss Elizabeth Ellison Charitable Trust

The Esme Mitchell Trust

Irish Linen Centre – Lisburn Museum

Environment and Heritage Service, Department of the Environment

The Belfast Society

The Marc Fitch Fund

PREFACE

The Living Linen Project was set up in 1995 in order to record as an Oral Archive the knowledge of the linen industry still available within a nucleus of people who were formerly working in the industry in Ulster. Over the period 1870 to 1970 the north east of Ireland was the world's leading linen producing area. Ulster manufacturers produced three quarters of the United Kingdom's output, specialising in the medium and fine end of the market. Concern has been expressed regarding the fact that despite the linen industry underpinning the local economy no comprehensive history of the industry over three centuries has been written. Nevertheless, considerable historical studies on the Irish linen industry in the eighteenth and nineteenth centuries have been published, but very little has been done in the last one hundred years to emphasise the world-wide nature of this trade in that period.

A very important feature of the linen industry in Ireland has been the resilience of the small or medium size private family firm. Although in the aftermath of the First World War, the difficulties of trade in the 1930s, and the Second World War, many of these companies were forced to close, a considerable number survived into the 1970s. However, by the close of the twentieth century there had been a very great reduction in numbers with less than twenty companies continuing to operate. Therefore, with the Irish linen trade in very steep decline, there appeared to be an urgent necessity to gather information while it was still available. The Living Linen project, in Phase I, was set up to gather knowledge quickly, which was held by many of the former owners and managers of the industry, since there was a wealth of information not put in writing. Nevertheless, there was also oral knowledge which could be recorded, from the representatives of the linen trade who travelled world wide and from pockets of highly skilled people living in manufacturing areas. This second group of recordings, with the work supported financially by the Heritage Lottery Fund from 1999 to 2002, constituted Phase II of the project and all Living Linen recordings were placed in the Ulster Folk & Transport Museum, Cultra, County Down.

Initially, in Phase I, various Living Linen committee members made, in the main, recordings of the owners and managers of the old linen industry. With others, I had the privilege of invitations to homes of linen merchants where, in some cases, records of their lifestyle, including portraits and photographs, going back over many years, were held. Many of the linen merchants built new properties or improved existing ones with the large growth of the linen industry in the nineteenth century in the Lagan Valley and particularly Belfast. It therefore appeared appropriate to compile a book concerned with a historical and architectural study of these houses.

In many ways, four families, the Charleys, the McCances, the Richardsons and the Barbours dominated, in the nineteenth century, the linen industry of the Lagan Valley between Lisburn and Belfast. With many members in each of these families established in their own houses it was felt necessary to give a short family history, associated with a family tree. Some of the properties have considerable architectural interest but equally other modest houses have strong associations with the linen industry. Unfortunately, some of the oldest and finest houses no longer exist but it has still proved possible to gather information and photographs regarding them. Although this book makes use of information and photographs gathered in the Living Linen project, it has had to draw on the considerable records of the Public Record Office of Northern Ireland, the Linen Hall Library and the Irish Linen Centre – Lisburn Museum.

INTRODUCTION

The Lagan Valley, stretching from Belfast to Lisburn and on to Blaris, Hillsborough and Dromore, is one of the most agriculturally fertile districts in Northern Ireland, and in the early seventeenth century it was one of the first to be settled in the plantation of Ulster, settlers coming principally from the north of England. For nearly two hundred and fifty years linen yarn and cloth were produced in great abundance in the Lagan Valley, during which time the industry dominated the economy of the area. Throughout the period capitalist development in Ulster's linen industry was linked to political and economic processes beyond its boundaries at the regional, national and international level. The seventeenth century Acts of Settlement saw the destruction of an Irish aristocracy and its replacement by another, but, alongside this, an economic revolution had begun. An English policy which helped lay the foundation for the linen industry in Ulster was the Cromwellian Settlement, which stimulated immigration from Britain. Immigrants from northern England settled in mid-Ulster, especially in the Lagan Valley and north Armagh, and here the linen industry developed along commercial lines based on the imported skills of the English linen weavers.

The 1650s onwards saw a significant group of Quakers, emigrating from northern England, who settled in small groups or as individual families in areas such as Lisburn, Lurgan, Magheralin, Banbridge and Moyallon. Indeed Quaker contributions to the formative stages of the linen industry came fifty years prior to the arrival of Louis Crommelin and the Huguenots in 1698. An important number of these French Protestant settlers, most of them skilled in the manufacture of fine linens and silk, came to Lisnagarvey, later known as Lisburn. Side by side with agriculture, the Lagan Valley developed the manufacture of fine linen and it was in the Lisburn area that the most important developments took place in the eighteenth century. Edward Wakefield writing in 1812 gives an account of the linen industry in County Down which had been flourishing for nearly a century:

> The whole tract is embellished with plantations, and whether owing to
> the wealth created by the linen manufacture, or the trade carried on at

Belfast and Newry, everything exhibits evident signs of increased population and industry. The banks of the rivers Bann and Lagan are covered with bleach fields, and present that cheerful pleasing scenery which characterises a manufacturing country and excites in the mind an idea of improved civilisation.

The river Lagan was a significant factor in the growth of the linen industry as was the Lagan Canal, constructed during the years 1756–1765, the engineer being Thomas Omer, who designed the whole canal, including the locks and lock keepers' houses. Thousands of tons of merchandise were imported and exported annually through Belfast and were transported by horse-drawn barge, and, since the path of the Canal lay in the Lagan Valley as far as Lisburn, nearly all the linen merchants had a private quay for the convenience of their works.

By the mid-eighteenth century the linen industry in the north of Ireland was firmly established and the fortunes of landlords, bleachers and drapers were dependent upon its continued expansion. The ten-mile stretch along the Lagan between Lisburn and Belfast had become renowned for its numerous bleach greens, many of which were run by settlers, although the earliest record of a bleach green is in 1626, established near Lambeg by John Williamson. A large segment of this powerful and wealthy group of bleachers was composed of Quakers who were also active in the Gilford and Banbridge area. In the late eighteenth and early nineteenth centuries the bleacher was the most important man in the linen industry leading a many-sided life, but primarily as a merchant. However, he was also an industrialist and frequently the owner of a country house and a small estate, living a life much like that of a landed gentleman. After 1825, the capital which had been accumulated by merchants, bleachers and drapers was invested in a variety of manufacturing establishments.

In Lisburn, William Coulson set up a linen damask business in 1764 which was ultimately to produce table linens for the British royal family and for the crowned heads of Europe. John Barbour settled near Lisburn in 1784 where he built a village, 'The Plantation', to house his workers and erected his business premises to make linen thread. With the increasing importance of water power William Barbour, John's son, moved the business to Hilden adding a spinning mill and establishing the basis for the largest thread manufactory in the world. Increasing prosperity, and the succeeding family generations, meant that the Barbour family both built new houses and bought estates. The village of Hilden grew according to the growth of William Barbour & Sons. It is interesting to reflect that Conway, one of the larger 'linen' houses, much associated with Sir Milne Barbour, was actually built by Edward Charley on land leased from the Seymour Hill estate.

Nearby at Lambeg, the Richardson family, originally all Quakers, took over the Glenmore bleachworks and eventually Glenmore House which had previously been owned by another linen family, the Williamsons. In the mid-nineteenth century the firm of Richardson Sons & Owden was one of the largest linen manufacturing firms in the world with extensive links throughout the globe, particularly in North and South America and in Canada. At Dunmurry, J. & W. Charley, one of the oldest linen families, were well-known bleachers and finishers, but also set up a factory at Seymour Hill, and were renowned for their very fine linens which were often commissioned by nobility.

Moving down the Lagan Valley towards Belfast another very old linen family were the McCances of Suffolk. They were merchants and bleachers who owned a wide tract of land south of the Antrim Plateau which included Colin Glen. John McCance, MP, had interests in public affairs and local government outside the family linen business. As a merchant banker he became chairman of the shareholders' committee from the time when the Bank of Montgomery, Orr & Sloane, in which he was a partner, was incorporated in 1824 to form the Northern Banking Company which for the linen industry was very important. The McCance family intermarried with the Charleys, the Russells and the Bristows so linking more houses with linen associations in the Lagan Valley.

By the 1860s the linen mill and factory owners in Ulster were, unlike the rest of Ireland, enjoying a period of prosperity due to the American Civil War, when demand for linen cloth soared due to the great reduction in the supply of cotton. Nonetheless, the linen industry has always been cyclical and it was so in the nineteenth century but it is also true that this period created the greatest wealth and provided the manufacturers with the resources to build interesting houses. Equally there were linen houses in the eighteenth century which were adapted and enlarged to suit their owners' affluent lifestyles. Many of the linen owners and their families lived close to their businesses in the Lagan Valley but others aspired to grand suburban villas within easy travelling distance of Lisburn or Belfast.

However, the linen merchants' houses which reflected their lifestyles have been largely forgotten and, unfortunately, a considerable number of them, such as Roseville, a fine Georgian house in Lisburn, have been knocked down. Nevertheless there still remain many of the original 'linen' houses which continue to contribute to life in the Lagan Valley, perhaps none more so than Ballydrain, now Malone Golf Club.

In this study the houses have been grouped into family ownership rather than geographical location in order to show the interconnections with the linen industry. Many of the linen families intermarried since they formed a small social elite, and this led to some of the 'linen' houses having a history spanning two important families, an example being Huntley, Dunmurry, built by the Hunter family, one of whom married into the Charley family, and latterly the house has been in the ownership of another linen family, the Brysons of Spence Bryson.

This story of the linen families and their houses in the Lagan Valley is recorded here in order that it may provide a picture of a past era in the Irish linen industry.

ABBREVIATIONS

BNL	*Belfast Newsletter*
BT	*Belfast Telegraph*
ECA	*Emily Charley Album*
ILC & LM	Irish Linen Centre & Lisburn Museum
LHS	Lisburn Historical Society
LL	Living Linen
MBR	Monuments and Buildings Record of Northern Ireland
PRONI	Public Record Office of Northern Ireland
NMGNI UFTM	Ulster Folk & Transport Museum
NMGNI UM	Ulster Museum
JFR	J.F. Rankin, Esq.

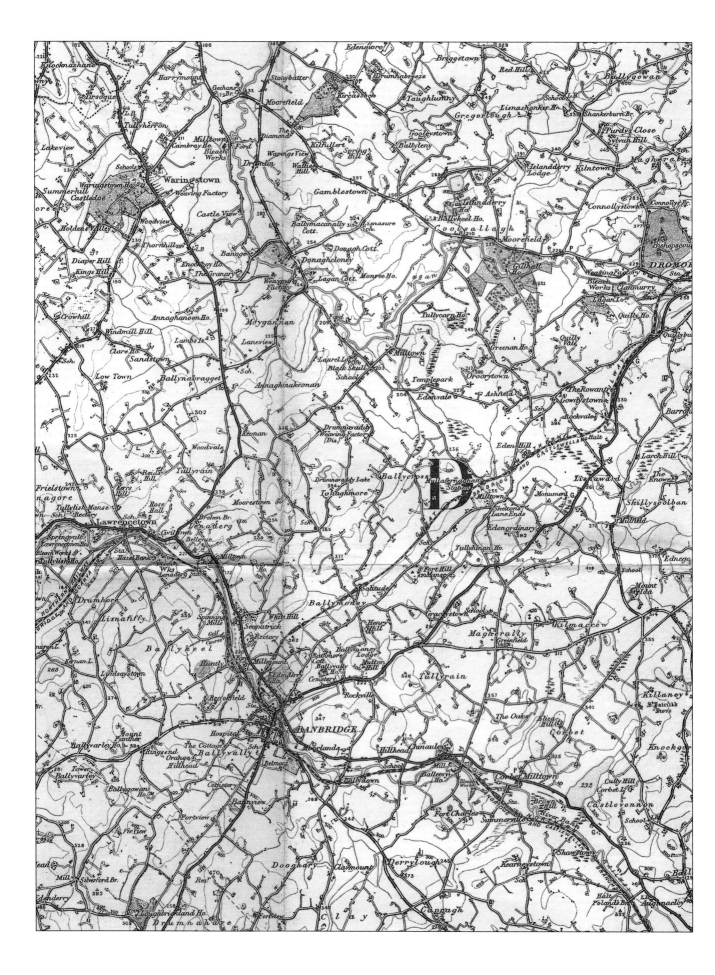

1

WARINGSTOWN,
DONAGHCLONEY
AND
DROMORE

Waringstown, County Down, 1849

Hugh Frazer

Reproduced with the kind permission of the National Museums and Galleries of Northern Ireland

WARINGSTOWN
HOUSE

Waringstown House

JFR

WARINGSTOWN HOUSE is situated between two and three miles south-east of Lurgan, Co. Armagh and is in the village in County Down which bears the family name of Waring. John Waring of Cherry Tree House near Chorley in Lancashire came to Ireland about 1600 and settled at Toome in County Antrim where he acquired land and established a tannery. He married Mary Peers, daughter of Rev. Peers of Derriaghy, Co. Antrim, and their eldest son William, after his father's death, purchased in 1658 half the parish of Donaghcloney. Waringstown House, built in 1667 by William Waring, is one of the earliest surviving unfortified Irish houses. Adjacent to the house were built the homes of his tenantry, most of whom came from the north of England, so establishing the village of Waringstown.

Waringstown House was built of land stone boulders set in a mortar of puddle clay and the roof was originally covered with oak shingles, which accounts

Side view of Waringstown House showing tall chimney stacks

MBR

Front doorway of Waringstown House

MBR

for the tall chimney heads designed to throw sparks from wood fuel clear of the roof. The southern view of the house, seen from the garden, is distinctly Dutch, with stepped gables and dormer lattice windows carrying their characteristic heads. Waringstown House is three stories high and is flanked by two-storey one-bay overlapping wings, the main frontage consisting of three bays, harled and coloured with terracotta-coloured lime and tallow. The external angles are finished with plain V-shaped channelled quoins with similar pilaster strips to the central bay. In 1834 the roof shingles were replaced with slates and at attic level the roof has a nineteenth-century modillioned cornice which is returned on the north and south gables. The central doorway is flanked by fluted pilasters on moulded bases on which rest an entablature, surmounted by a triangular pediment. The interior of the house has many Jacobean features, including the magnificent oak staircase, and the flooring consists of wide oak boards which may be the original timber sawn from the surrounding woods, but the majority of the fittings are nineteenth century.

During the Williamite Wars, William Waring, fearing that his estate, derived from the Act of Settlement, would be confiscated, and that he would be killed, fled with his family to Douglas in the Isle of Man leaving his house in charge of his servants. In the Warings' absence, the Duke of Schomberg is said to have occupied Waringstown House, and a room is still known as the 'Duke's Room'.

However, in 1691 peace was established and William Waring returned to Waringstown.

Whilst the family was in the Isle of Man, William's eldest son Samuel Waring set out on a tour of Flanders and the Low Countries, about the year 1688, where he viewed the weaving of diaper and other fine fabric of a size and quality much superior to the then current Irish linen. There is a strong local tradition that after the death of his father Samuel Waring persuaded a colony of Flemish weavers to leave their homeland and settle in and around the village of Waringstown. Eventually a large contingent of weavers originating from the neighbourhood of Cambray settled in and around Moira, Lurgan and Portadown. These people brought with them looms adapted to the weaving of cambric and fine broadcloth, and were, along with the Huguenots of Lisburn, the earliest weavers of cambric in Ireland.

Samuel Waring continued to encourage the development of the linen industry and was one of the original trustees of the Linen Board, formed in 1711. The manufacture of linen quickly spread in the area and by 1744, Harris, in his history of County Down, wrote of Waringstown:

> In this town and neighbourhood of it the linen manufacture is carried on to great advantage, where it was introduced and cherished by the late Samuel Waring, Esq., well known for the great services he has done his country in this trade; which has spread so considerably here since that time, that a colony of fine diaper weavers was transplanted lately from hence to Dundalk.

William Waring, *c* 1695 (1619–1703)

JFR

Elizabeth Lewis, writing in *Textile History*, 1984, Vol 15, 'An 18th century linen damask tablecloth from Ireland', has described a remarkable damask tablecloth discovered among the civic regalia of the City of Winchester in England. The cloth is of damask and is eleven feet long by nine feet wide woven in one piece, and on the cloth one may read the words:

> The Coronation and inauguration of George Augustus, King of Great Britain, France and Ireland, Defender of the Faith – God Save King George – 1717 – Wrought in Warringstown in the County of Down in the north of Ireland.

This cloth, thought to have been woven in 1727, and now in the keeping of the Irish Linen Centre – Lisburn Museum, has an enormously intricate design showing the coronation procession of George I and a map of London. Elizabeth Lewis, sometime curator of the Winchester Museums' Service, has established that it is almost certain that the Waringstown weavers used pamphlets which had been prepared for the coronation in London as the source of their design woven in the cloth. However, as Lewis states, 'The circumstances

Samuel Waring, *c* 1720, (1660–1739), who established the linen industry

JFR

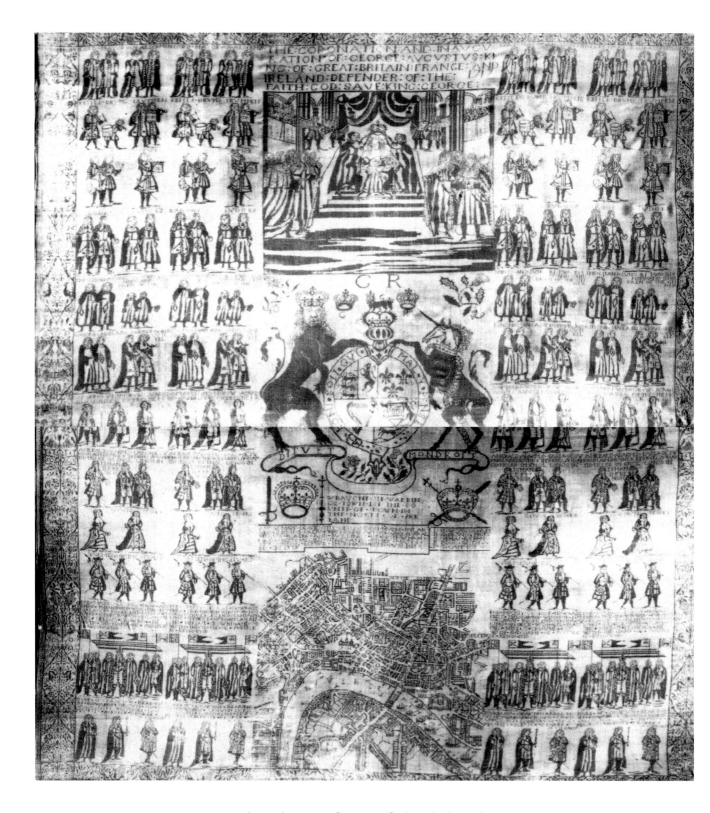

The 18th century
Waringstown tablecloth
Winchester City Museum

surrounding the manufacture of the cloth and its subsequent arrival in Winchester can only be guessed at.' Nevertheless, she does put forward a possible explanation, supported by the references to the place of origin and to the weaving trade, that it was a *chef d'oeuvre* designed and presented by the linen industry under Samuel Waring as a gesture of loyalty to the Crown and as a demonstration of the weavers' skill.

The production of fine linen continued and by 1886 there were between three and four hundred handloom weavers living in Waringstown and neighbourhood, their cambrics and damasks being considered to be of very high quality. Linen manufacture, both power loom and even a small amount of hand loom, was conducted in Waringstown until the late 1950s and was the main source of employment for the village.

Waringstown House was occupied by members of the Waring family until the death of Mrs D.G. Waring in 1968, after which the house stood empty for a period, but at present it is again occupied by a descendant of the original family, Mr Michael Harnett.

Waringstown, 1703 AD, from a map by Francis Nevil, Esq., Collector of her Majesty's Revenue
PRONI

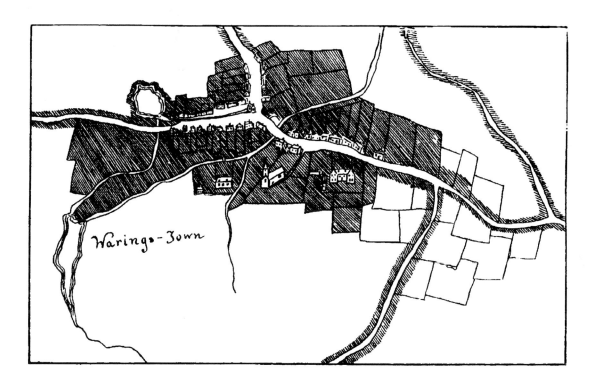

LIDDELL FAMILY TREE

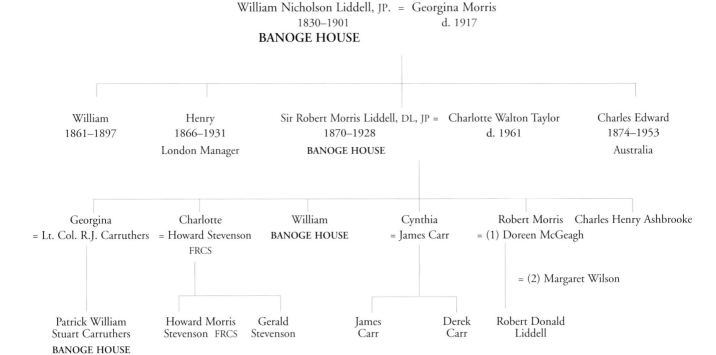

William Nicholson Liddell, JP. = Georgina Morris
1830–1901   d. 1917
BANOGE HOUSE

William
1861–1897

Henry
1866–1931
London Manager

Sir Robert Morris Liddell, DL, JP = Charlotte Walton Taylor
1870–1928   d. 1961
BANOGE HOUSE

Charles Edward
1874–1953
Australia

Georgina
= Lt. Col. R.J. Carruthers

Charlotte
= Howard Stevenson
FRCS

William
BANOGE HOUSE

Cynthia
= James Carr

Robert Morris
= (1) Doreen McGeagh

= (2) Margaret Wilson

Charles Henry Ashbrooke

Patrick William
Stuart Carruthers
BANOGE HOUSE

Howard Morris
Stevenson FRCS

Gerald
Stevenson

James
Carr

Derek
Carr

Robert Donald
Liddell

BANOGE
HOUSE

Banoge House
JFR

BANOGE HOUSE, DONAGHCLONEY, was, for more than a century and a half, the family home of the Liddells, whose company, William Liddell & Sons manufactured very fine linen damask and cambrics. The river Lagan is crossed by an ancient two-arched bridge in the immediate vicinity of Banoge House and close to the bridge is Banoge Mill, built originally by Robert Patterson, a linen draper, for the milling of flour in 1764. In 1836 William Nicholson acquired Banoge House and Banoge Mill, converting the latter into a works for bleaching and beetling linen. At this time only the front part of Banoge House was built and the Ordnance Survey map of 1835 shows a small bleach green where the garden of the present house is situated.

To the front, which is late eighteenth century, Banoge is a two-storey, six-bay house, the exterior of which is stuccoed. The roof is slated with overhanging eaves and the house has stepped quoins at each corner. The front door is sheltered by a porch which itself is topped by a small balustrade. At right angles to the building is a nineteenth-century extension built in a similar style to the

original but with the upper and lower stories separated by a string course. There is a small two-storey extension to the right of the main building with its roof at a lower level and this may be part of the original house on the site. William Nicholson carried out a considerable planting of trees on his lands in 1851, including birch, lime, laburnum, mountain ash, sycamore, poplar, beech and oak, and some of these may be seen around the house.

William Nicholson Liddell, a great-nephew of William Nicholson, served his apprenticeship in the Nicholson business, and when his great-uncle retired in 1855 he offered the lease on Banoge bleach green to William Liddell, who was then twenty-five years old. However, he required sufficient capital to finance not only the bleach green but the purchase of yarn and cloth and he set up a financial partnership with John Shaw Brown and a Lurgan man named Magee. The manager of the bleach green, a man called Stewart, lived in Banoge House, at that time consisting only of the front part of the later building.

In 1859 William Liddell married Georgina Morris, daughter of a successful Lurgan solicitor, and they set up home in the town. Georgina presented her husband with £1,000 which enabled him, and his friend John Shaw Brown, to buy out their partner Magee. William appointed his brother-in-law Thomas Morris to manage the bleach green and this young man went to live in Banoge House.

The 1860s was, perhaps, the most prosperous decade in the history of the

linen trade, owing to the American Civil War creating an acute shortage of cotton and the subsequent unprecedented demand for linen. By 1864 William Liddell had opened the Belfast office of Brown and Liddell and he and his wife lived at 3, Windsor Avenue, Belfast. However, with the continuing boom in linen sales, William Liddell terminated his partnership with John Shaw Brown in 1866, setting up his own business and moving his family to a renovated Banoge House. Over the next twenty years the business grew appreciably and, by 1890, Banoge House had been enlarged and modernised.

William Nicholson Liddell died in 1901 and was succeeded by his third son, Robert Morris Liddell, who had been living in New York and managing the American branch of the business. Robert Liddell with his wife and young family moved into Banoge House in 1902. At this period the inside staff at the house consisted of a butler, cook, parlour-maid, housemaid, nurse and nursemaid, and the outside staff included a coachman and groom, two chauffeurs, two gardeners, a cowman and several men who worked in the fields.

Sir Robert Morris Liddell, DL, JP, was knighted in 1916 for very considerable services in raising money for the Ulster Volunteer Force Hospital which was opened in 1915 and also for support for the UVF Patriotic Fund which gave help to men in the army and navy wounded in the War and unable to support themselves and their families. In the same year Sir Robert and Lady Liddell decided

Iveagh Harriers, Master and hounds at Banoge House, 31 January 1903
Private Collection

Sir Robert Liddell
Private Collection

11

to enlarge Banoge House by the addition of an oak-panelled smokeroom, a large guest room and a bedroom for their eldest son, William, who had just started to serve an apprenticeship in the factory. Sir Robert Liddell died in 1928 in his 58th year; however, his forty years in business were years of prosperity and progress in the linen industry. Banoge House continued in Liddell family ownership until the late 1960s when it was sold.

The relatively modern village of Donaghcloney grew up around the large damask factory of William Liddell & Sons, occupying a site on a meadow beside the river Lagan. In fact the community was centred around the factory with the company owning many workers' houses in the village, running the school, and employing the doctor who had his surgery at the top of the factory path.   In 1894 the Church of St Patrick, a small iron church, was presented by William Liddell to meet the needs of the rapidly increasing population in Donaghcloney. This continued in use until 1980, when the schoolhouse, erected in 1903, was made available and consecrated for use as a church. Sport was encouraged in the village and the Liddells acted for many years as patrons of the Donaghcloney Cricket Club, which still runs to the present day.

Sir Robert and Lady Liddell with their family at Banoge House c 1926

Private Collection

CAMBRAY
HOUSE

CAMBRAY HOUSE is situated north of Waringstown village and was built *c* 1840 by John Henning, then owner of the linen works of John Henning & Son, Ltd. Sir Charles Lanyon, the architect of Waringstown Presbyterian Church, is reputed also to be the architect of Cambray House built some ten years earlier. A four square, two-storey house, the building is rendered with Italianate detailing and has a slate roof. The entrance front has a projecting square portico, and the house has tall Georgian-glazed windows, triple above the porch. The interior contains some fine plaster work.

From early in the nineteenth century an industry in the weaving of cambric was growing up around Lurgan, Dromore and Waringstown. Amongst the earliest of these to undertake the weaving of cambric on a large scale were Thomas and George McMurray of Waringstown. According to Bassett in *County Down 100 Years Ago*, the firm had been established in Waringstown by George McMurray, about the year 1750, for hand-loom cambric weaving. By 1817, they were using seventy looms and had 300 employees. This is confirmed by Atkinson writing in 1823 about Waringstown:

Cambray House

JFR

13

Lettering above the doorway of the old linen weaving factory of John Henning and Son Limited

JFR

This interesting village, which forms a feature of distinction on the estate of Richard Holt Waring, Esq. is known on the western plains of Downshire, by its rural beauty, and distinguished in the commercial history of the county, by the respectable and long established cambric manufactory of Messrs. George McMurray and Son. Here 70 looms, furnishing employment to 300 hands, are engaged in the production of cambrics, which sell in the brown state …

John Henning appears to have worked with the McMurrays, but in 1827 when Thomas McMurray moved to Dromore, he took over their cambric weaving business in Waringstown. Additionally, in 1836, a trade in hemstitched cambric handkerchiefs was set up by John Henning in Waringstown, providing a new source of employment for the women of the area. This trade became highly successful and, in the Great Exhibition of 1851, John Henning was awarded a gold medal by the judges of textiles, and was the only manufacturer in the United Kingdom to receive a medal for cambric.

The doorway of Cambray House

MBR

The business and factory of John Henning & Son, Damask Manufacturers, at Waringstown, was acquired by Walpole Brothers, linen merchants, London and Dublin, in 1889. At the same time a small factory was opened at Lurgan for hemming and hemstitching, which, at a later date, was removed to Clarence Street, Belfast. Hennings were famed for their very fine quality linens, which were all hand woven, and in buying the factory Walpoles gained an entry to linen weaving. Walpoles built a power loom factory in Waringstown, which continued to be known as John Henning & Son, in 1906, but they also continued the handloom business which was practically all damask. Gradually this business decreased and during World War II the factory produced aeroplane linen. Walpoles manufactured linen in Waringstown until the early 1960s when the factory was converted to making boilers.

John Henning, of Cambray House, died in 1874 and his widow and son David continued to occupy the house until 1902 when it passed out of Henning ownership.

LAGAN LODGE

LAGAN LODGE was built by Thomas McMurray soon after he came to Dromore from Waringstown in 1827. The house, which is roughcast and whitewashed with hipped roof, is in the cottage style, one storey and basement at the front and two storey at the rear. Lagan Lodge is a listed Georgian country house which still retains many of the original architectural details including high corniced ceilings in the main reception rooms, ornate fireplaces, and sliding sash windows with window shutters. The accommodation includes a spacious reception hall, three reception rooms, six bedrooms, former staff accommodation, kitchen and store rooms. Originally a wing was built on to the house to serve as a pay office for the weavers and there was a lapping room in the yard.

Thomas McMurray settled in Dromore in 1827 and pioneered the cambric handkerchief trade, which was slow to start but after 1831, with Ulster mill spun yarns becoming available, a great impetus was given to cambric manufacture. The business of Thomas McMurray & Co. became highly successful in the manufacture of linen which they also bleached and finished, having agencies for the sale of their goods in London and Paris.

Lagan Lodge
JFR

15

The architecture of Henry Hobart and Samuel Heron was important in the context of many of the late nineteenth and early twentieth century linen houses. Henry Hobart's father had married into the McMurray family and he was born at Lagan Lodge on Christmas Eve 1858. After his education at the Royal Belfast Academical Institution he was apprenticed to William Lynn and in 1890 he returned home to Lagan Lodge where he set up his practice in a wonderfully light-filled room which had been used by his father in connection with his linen business. In 1904 he went into partnership with Samuel Heron and the firm moved to Belfast, completing orders for churches, houses and businesses. One of Henry Hobart's early commissions in connection with the linen industry was for Messrs Murphy & Stevenson Ltd in 1896 when he designed a row of red brick terrace houses in Dromore, and in 1907 he designed alterations and additions to the weaving factory for the same firm. Lagan Lodge remained in the possession of the Hobart family until 1999.

CLANMURRY

CLANMURRY is situated on Lower Quilly Road, Dromore, Co. Down, in grounds of about five acres and adjacent to the new main Hillsborough-Banbridge Road. Dating from about 1830 and built by William McClelland, Clanmurry is a fine example of a Georgian house with decorative plaster work and well proportioned rooms. The accommodation consists of library, drawing room, dining room, cloakroom and kitchen on the ground floor with six bed-rooms and two bathrooms on the first floor. The main avenue, which has a gate lodge (now boarded up) at the entrance, leads from the Lower Quilly Road to a sweep in front of the house. On the south side a porticoed verandah overlooks a terrace and inset flower beds leading to a semi-circular garden with goldfish pond. At the rear there is a partially walled garden in lawns and flower beds with a summer house, greenhouse and potting shed, and, in addition, there is a sep-arate vegetable and soft fruit garden with greenhouse. At the back of the house there is an enclosed yard with two lofted ranges of out-buildings consisting of stores, stables, workshops and garages. A back avenue leads from the yard to the Lower Quilly Road.

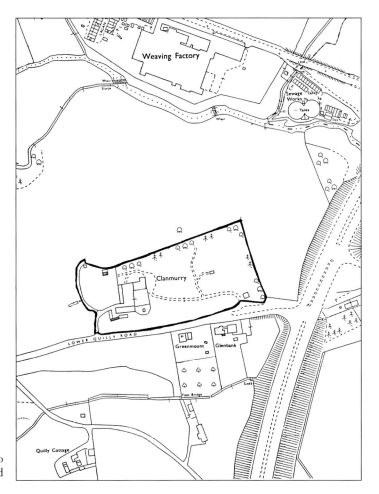

Clanmurry Estate, situated close to
the Dromore/Banbridge Road

William McClelland was a son-in-law of Thomas McMurray, owner of the
linen company Thomas McMurray & Co., which was established in Dromore
in 1827, and he worked in the company. On the death of Thomas McMurray
the company was run by his son William, and by William McClelland, who died
about 1865. Clanmurry was then occupied by another Dromore linen manufacturer, William Jardine, whose firm was established about 1843 for the weaving of fine and coarse linens with hand-looms. In 1868 the company
commenced the machine manufacture of linen shirt fronts and later set up a
complete department for the hemstitching and embroidering of fancy handkerchiefs, which were sold principally in Belfast and Glasgow. William Jardine &
Co. also owned a yarn bleach works at Quilly, which occupied the site of a
beetling mill, previously owned by the McMurrays. William Sprott & Co. of
Dromore owned the bleach works for some years and were succeeded by the
Jardines. In the twentieth century William Jardine & Co. passed into the ownership of Charles and John Baxter who were the great-grandsons of William
Jardine, but the company closed in 1963.

Clanmurry was occupied by the Jardine family until the mid-1920s when it

came into the possession of the Baxter family, who were solicitors in Dromore. They remained at Clanmurry for a further sixty years. The house was finally sold in the 1980s.

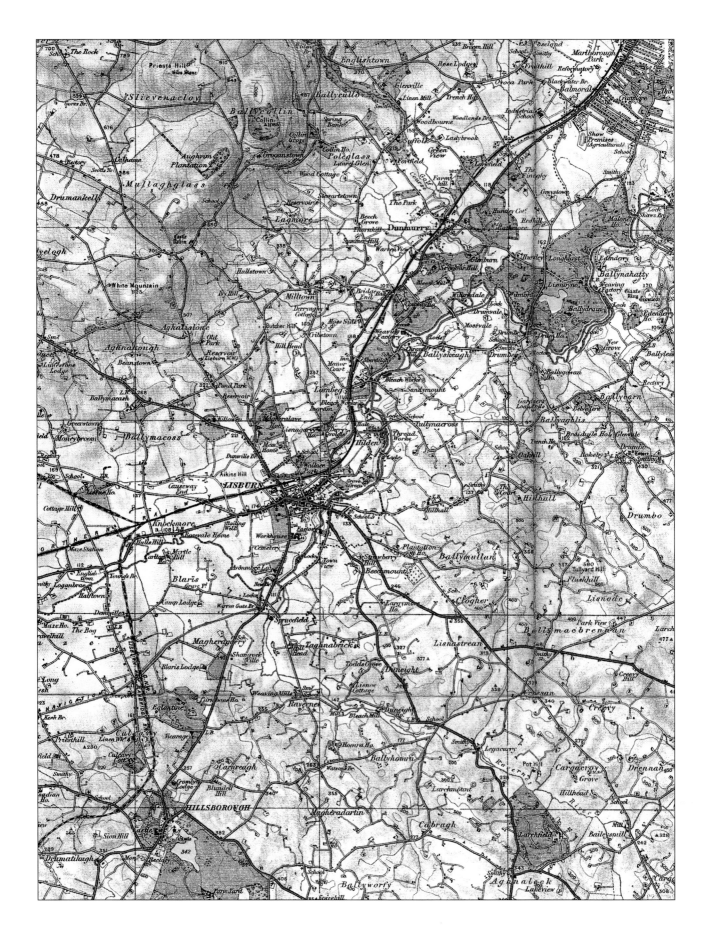

2
HILLSBOROUGH

View near Hillsborough, 1783

William Hincks

Reproduced with the kind permission of the Linen Hall Library

THE MULHOLLANDS
OF BELFAST

During the seventeenth century Ulster had a considerable linen industry but this was a domestic industry with spinning and weaving taking place mainly on farms and in villages, indeed it was dominated by the spinning wheel and the hand loom. In Belfast from the late 1770s mills began to be built for the spinning of cotton and by 1825 there were about 20 cotton mills centred on the Smithfield area of Belfast, making the spinning and weaving of cotton the principal textile industry.

Thomas Mulholland (1756–1820), the founder of the firm that was to become York Street Flax Spinning Company, appears to have conducted a prosperous muslin manufacturing business in Belfast at the end of the eighteenth century. About 1815 the firm of McCammon, Milford & Bailey, cotton spinners of Winetavern Street decided to sell their mill. Thomas Mulholland entered into partnership with John Hind, who was the son of a prominent Manchester cotton spinner, to buy the Winetavern Street mill and the new firm prospered. Thomas died in 1820 leaving five sons, Thomas (1786–1830), Andrew (1792–1866), John, William, who went to the West Indies, and St Clair

Kelburn (1798–1872). The Winetavern Street mill succeeded so well that the firm acquired additional premises in Francis Street nearby, where they erected some of the newly invented power looms for weaving cotton. In 1822 the Mulholland brothers and John Hind erected what was at the time considered a huge cotton mill in the Point Field near York Street. John Hind superintended the technical side of the business, and the brothers Mulholland, the mercantile side.

In 1825 James Kay of Preston invented a wet spinning process in that he discovered that a thorough soaking in cold water made flax fibres more slippery so that they could be drawn by machinery into a very fine yarn. This led to Kay and others erecting a large wet-spinning mill at Leeds, which was quickly followed by others at Nidderdale. Subsequently the brothers Mulholland were much impressed by the steady increase in shipments of flax from Belfast consigned to Leeds and the corresponding growth in the imports of yarn from the same area. In Ireland the hand spinning industry was quickly being undermined by these imports, and great distress arose in many districts removing a prop from the rural economy. Meanwhile in 1828, James Murland erected a wet spinning mill at Annsborough, Castlewellan, Co. Down and was the first in Ireland to produce linen yarn in appreciable quantity by power spinning. It was found that a properly equipped spinning mill could produce yarn of better quality at a much lower price than could be made by hand.

Mulholland's cotton mill at York Street was destroyed by fire in the summer of 1828 but by then the firm had already realised that the competition of Lancashire and Glasgow, where raw cotton was imported direct, was steadily growing and they anticipated that cotton spinning in Ireland was doomed. On the other hand, the exports of flax from Ireland to England and the importation of the yarns to be woven in Ireland equally put English flax spinners at a corresponding disadvantage. The profits in prospect for Irish mills were very tempting since the flax and the market for yarn were in Ulster, whereas the English spinners had to pay freight both ways at a time when no railways and only sailing ships were available. The Mulhollands built a new steam power mill in York Street beside the ruins of the old mill and it started work in 1830. Andrew Mulholland employed the young architect Thomas Jackson, newly arrived in Belfast, to design the York Street Spinning Mills. The Francis Street mill continued operations until at least the 1840s.

On the death of Thomas Mulholland senior he left the business to his two older sons, Thomas and Andrew, providing otherwise for John, William, St Clair and their sisters. Thomas lived only to see the new flax spinning mill started, dying in 1830 unmarried. The business was ably carried on by his brother Andrew who continued to trade as T. & A. Mulholland, Muslin Manufacturers, Union Street, until about 1840 when he took his son John (1819–1895) into partnership and the firm became Andrew Mulholland & Son. In 1846 Andrew Mulholland, having purchased the estate of Springvale, County Down from the

Matthew family, retired from the firm leaving John as sole proprietor. Andrew Mulholland added to the palatial residence at Springvale, then recently built by the Matthews, and now known as Ballywalter Park.

In 1852 the Mulhollands' great York Street mill employed 800 workers and had 16,000 spindles, spinning 700 tons of flax into yarn in a year. The Mulhollands made enormous profits from their wet spinning mill and others were quick to follow so that by 1850 there were twenty-nine mills in Belfast spinning flax compared to only four spinning cotton and in 1851 John Mulholland changed the name of the firm to the York Street Flax Spinning Company. On becoming proprietor of the firm John Mulholland took in, as managing partner, his brother-in-law Nicholas de la Cherois Crommelin who retired in 1860 and was followed by Mr Ogilvie Blair Graham, a native of Belfast, who had acquired a fortune in New Orleans.

Linens rapidly took the place of cotton textiles when the American Civil War (1861–1865) cut off the supply of raw cotton to Great Britain and the Ulster linen industry expanded dramatically. John Mulholland, who had political ambitions, decided in 1864 to turn his firm into a Limited Liability Company, retaining a large holding of shares which eventually passed to his descendants, but meanwhile making immense profits in the American War boom. The Company extended its operations and opened branches in Paris (1870), New York (1871), London (1874), Berlin (1876) and Melbourne (1882). Expansion continued with new mills and a weaving factory being built in York Street; other mills were purchased and the Muckamore bleachworks near Antrim was purchased in 1883 making the Company totally vertically integrated.

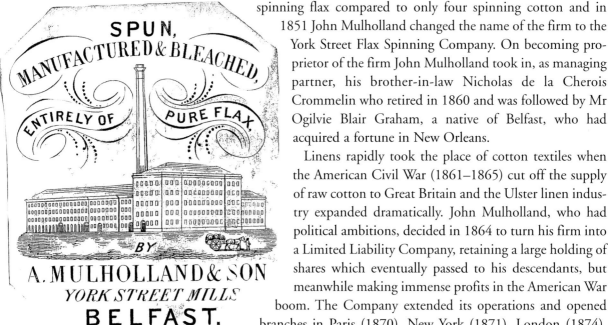

A. Mulholland and Son,
linen stamp
NMGNI UM

In less than a century after Thomas Mulholland founded the firm, his grandson saw it achieve the position of the largest company of flax spinners, linen manufacturers and distributors in the world. After the formation of the York Street Flax Spinning Co. Ltd, John Mulholland sat as MP for Downpatrick from 1874 to 1885, having purchased from David Ker the Southwell (Downpatrick) estate. He was raised to the peerage in 1892 as Baron Dunleath, choosing the title from the ancient name of Downpatrick, and was succeeded in 1895 by his only surviving son Henry Lyle, and thereafter by the 3rd, 4th, 5th and 6th Barons.

York Street Flax Spinning Company was large enough to weather the many cyclical swings of the Irish linen industry through both the First and Second World Wars. The York Street Mill was destroyed by German incendiaries in the blitz of Belfast, 4/5 May 1941, and was the largest fire ever seen in the city. However, after the war the York Street Mill was rebuilt but the linen trade decreased in the second half of the twentieth century as synthetic textiles took over and lifestyles changed. In the 1950s industrial consultants in time and motion were called into the company to try and increase production but the real difficulty was that linen had gone out of fashion and was also too expensive. The resolution to close the company was taken on 18 May 1961 and the York Street Flax Spinning Company was closed down on 1 February 1962.

MULHOLLAND FAMILY TREE

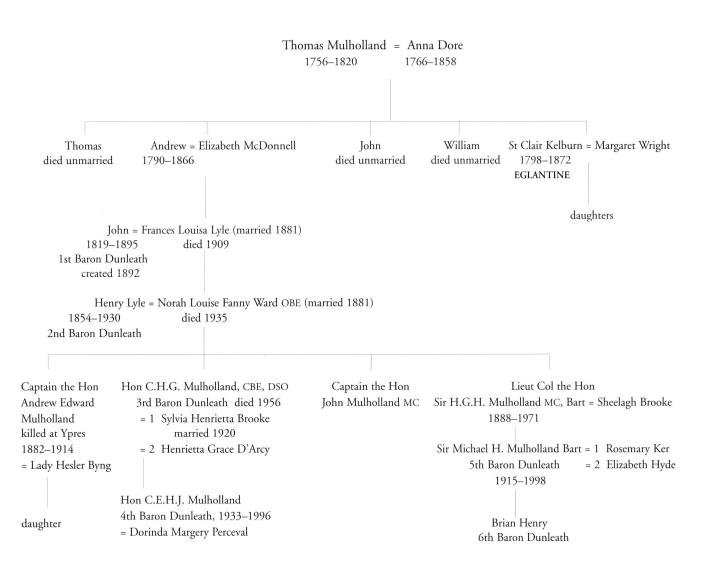

Thomas Mulholland = Anna Dore
1756–1820   1766–1858

Thomas
died unmarried

Andrew = Elizabeth McDonnell
1790–1866

John
died unmarried

William
died unmarried

St Clair Kelburn = Margaret Wright
1798–1872
EGLANTINE

daughters

John = Frances Louisa Lyle (married 1881)
1819–1895   died 1909
1st Baron Dunleath
created 1892

Henry Lyle = Norah Louise Fanny Ward OBE (married 1881)
1854–1930   died 1935
2nd Baron Dunleath

Captain the Hon
Andrew Edward
Mulholland
killed at Ypres
1882–1914
= Lady Hesler Byng

daughter

Hon C.H.G. Mulholland, CBE, DSO
3rd Baron Dunleath died 1956
= 1 Sylvia Henrietta Brooke
married 1920
= 2 Henrietta Grace D'Arcy

Hon C.E.H.J. Mulholland
4th Baron Dunleath, 1933–1996
= Dorinda Margery Perceval

Captain the Hon
John Mulholland MC

Lieut Col the Hon
Sir H.G.H. Mulholland MC, Bart = Sheelagh Brooke
1888–1971

Sir Michael H. Mulholland Bart = 1 Rosemary Ker
5th Baron Dunleath   = 2 Elizabeth Hyde
1915–1998

Brian Henry
6th Baron Dunleath

EGLANTINE
HOUSE

Eglantine House

MBR

EGLANTINE HOUSE was situated almost midway between Lisburn and Hillsborough on the main Lisburn to Dublin road. In 1837 the *Ordnance Survey Memoirs* record for the Parish of Blaris a Gentleman's Residence, Eglantine, the residence of Hugh Moore, Esquire, situated in the townland of Carnbane. Atkinson, writing some years prior to this, in 1823, also mentions Hugh Moore, Esq. as the owner and remarks on the elegant arrangement of the Eglantine gate, avenue and plantations. The Moore family had come from Ayrshire, one branch settling at Mount Panther, Co. Down and the other at Eglantine House, Hillsborough. Eglantine was built as a dower house for the Hill family of Hillsborough but not occupied. In the early 1820s Hugh Moore was the first owner but he was followed by St Clair Kelburn Mulholland, youngest son of Thomas Mulholland. The demesne of one hundred and twenty acres was leased in 1841 from the Downshire estate and Charles Lanyon employed as architect to reface and improve the house. Lanyon refaced the house

The staircase of Eglantine House
MBR

in neo-classical style with a central projecting open Doric porch, refurbished the interior, and replaced the two old gate lodges. The 1861 valuation describes Eglantine as a very elegant mansion, large and commodious with extensive offices attached.

The house, on two floors with cellars, incorporated a late eighteenth century structure, but in its later form was of the mid-nineteenth century. Eglantine was a square built house, containing at ground level a large stair hall, enclosed by reception rooms on three sides; in these rooms were a number of marble chimney pieces of late eighteenth-century character. The main feature of interest was the stair with cantilevered stone treads with shaped ends, and ramped handrail with wrought iron balusters; it was presumably of mid-nineteenth-century construction. The stair rose in two curving flights, meeting at a half-landing, where two short flights diverged and rose to the first floor landing, which had a central oval ceiling light.

St Clair Kelburn Mulholland, JP, impressed by the success of his brother Andrew's new spinning mill, York Street Flax Spinning Company, decided in 1833 to build another spinning mill. He approached John Hind, then a partner of Captain Boyd in the Blackstaff mill, with a view to a partnership which was arranged, the capital being half and half and trading as S.K. Mulholland and Hind. The mill was built behind the Academical Institution in College Square, Belfast and years later it became the Durham Street Weaving Company.

EGLANTINE HOUSE
1868

LANDSTEWARD BARNES	ANNE STOBART	REV H. STOBART	
ST CLAIR K. MULHOLLAND	JANE MULHOLLAND	MISS J. WRIGHT	
& HIS WIFE	2 CHILDREN	2 CHILDREN	EMILY MULHOLLAND
MRS M. MULHOLLAND		MARY F. MULHOLLAND	2 CHILDREN
GRANDSON			

THE 7 CHILDREN ARE STOBARTS

Private Collection

In 1850 St Clair K. Mulholland retired from the linen trade to his residence Eglantine, and died in 1872 being survived by his wife and daughters. Eglantine Parish Church was built in his memory by Mrs Mulholland and members of the family on the lands of Eglantine, within five minutes' walk of Newport Bridge, and the church was consecrated in 1875. The house continued to be occupied by Mulhollands until 1918 when the last remaining daughter of St Clair Mulholland died.

Eglantine House was then bought by E.T. Green, who was a well known figure in the agricultural and commercial life of Ulster and had built up a highly successful business as a manufacturer and distributor of animal feeding stuffs. Subsequently, Eglantine was occupied by his son Professor E.R.R. Green, Director of the Institute of Irish Studies, Queen's University, Belfast, 1970–1981. Rodney Green will be remembered as an economic and social historian whose book, *The Lagan Valley, 1800–50*, sets out the local history of the industrial revolution in the context of the Lagan Valley and the development of the linen industry. E.R.R. Green also made a study of industrial archaeology and published *The Industrial Archaeology of County Down*, a definitive work which included a major section on the linen industry.

The final occupant of Eglantine was Saxon Tate, the first permanent Chief Executive of the Industrial Development Board of Northern Ireland, who held the post for three years. Eglantine remained unoccupied for some years and was discussed by Lisburn Borough Council as suitable for new Council Headquarters but unfortunately in the period 1987–1988 the house was set on fire and totally destroyed.

LARCHFIELD
HOUSE

Larchfield House

JFR

THE LARCHFIELD ESTATE, the majority of which lies within a stone-built demesne wall at Baillies Mills, Co. Down, is twelve miles south-west of Belfast. William Mussenden, Esq., DL, JP, a major Belfast merchant, bought it about 1750 and built the original house which had the front door facing west. Early records show Lord Bristol, Bishop of Derry, as having stayed there in 1783. The attractive Georgian house with its sweeping lawns, gardens and backcloth of rolling agricultural land and parkland trees, is placed in the centre of the Estate. The rear of the house looks out across lawns and formal gardens to a woodland garden, which falls away to a fish pond having a background of rhododendrons and giant silver firs.

Larchfield was sold by the Mussenden family in 1868 to Ogilvie Graham, Esq., DL, who built on a new south front and added an extension to the rear in 1885. The principal accommodation consists of, on the ground floor, three reception rooms, drawing room, dining room and library with an attractive hall, all facing south, and on the first floor eight main bedrooms and three bathrooms. Adjoining the house is a well built stable yard giving accommodation for a number of carriages as well as providing stabling and storage. The well planted formal gardens lead on to a walled garden containing a vinery, greenhouses, peach house and potting sheds. Larchfield Estate also contains two farm houses, two gate lodges and a gamekeeper's house.

Ogilvie Blair Graham, DL, JP (1820–1897), married in 1861 Louise Sarah daughter of Ambrose Lanfear of New Orleans, USA, who inherited considerable wealth. Ogilvie Graham became a managing partner in the York Street Flax Spinning Company when it was a very thriving business. His son Ogilvie Blair Graham, DL (1865–1928) married Grace Cottnam, daughter of Rt Hon. John Young of Galgorm Castle, Co. Antrim and continued to live at Larchfield. Again he was succeeded in Larchfield by his son Lt Col. Ogilvie Blair Graham, DSO, OBE, DL, born 1891, who became a senior managing director of York Street Flax Spinning Mill.

Larchfield was sold in 1968 to Leslie Mackie, Esq., and again the house had an owner with a connection to the linen trade. James Mackie & Sons not only serviced the British spinning and weaving industry but as the European market developed in the twentieth century and the textile trade flourished Mackie's patented machines were shipped around the globe. Larchfield remains in Leslie Mackie's ownership.

CULCAVY COTTAGE

CULCAVY COTTAGE was situated about a mile north of Hillsborough, on a site adjacent to the Hillsborough Linen Company, Limited. Many of the linen weaving factories were built on the sites of older enterprises which used water power and the buildings belonging to the Hillsborough Linen Company were erected on a site which had originally served the purposes of a distillery. This had been built in 1826 by Hercules Bradshaw, and continued in existence until his death about 1860 when it was converted into the Hillsborough Woollen Company. In 1876 a further change was made from wool to linens, the company reorganised and the name changed to the Hillsborough Linen Co., Ltd, which was owned by the Richardsons, Pims and other shareholders. Mr J.J. Pim of Lisburn was Managing Director and Mr Arthur Pim, Secretary, resided at Culcavy Cottage. The Hillsborough Linen Co., Ltd operated successfully for many years and in 1917 was bought from the Richardsons by the Cowdy/Pringle family who ran it until it closed in 1965.

A description of the house is given in the *Archaeological Survey of County Down*:

Culcavy Cottage, Hillsborough, built of rubble with brick dressings, rendered

Arthur Pim, Esq.
Secretary of the Hillsborough
Linen Company Limited, 1899

and colour washed and of one and two storeys, was probably built *c.* 1826. The single storey block, with attics lighted by dormer windows was approximately of U-plan, with wings projecting on the south to flank a central recessed bay. The east wing extended to the two-storey block on the north which was rectangular in plan. A shallow veranda (seen in the photograph) extended the full width of the south and east frontages of the single-storey block. The entrance was in the east wing having a semi-elliptical arched fanlight and narrow side lights. Extending to cover the verandas, the roofs were shallow pitched, slated or lead covered, the two-storey block having wide eaves with shaped brackets.

Griffith, in his valuation of 1863, records a gate lodge at Culcavy Cottage, and both houses had a delightful situation overlooking a lake, in well planted grounds. The house and lodge were demolished in the 1950s and a new house built in the grounds.

Opposite and below:
Views of Culcavy Cottage in the 1890s when the Pim family was in residence
Private Collection

OGLES GROVE

Ogles Grove 1904/5

PRONI

AS EARLY AS 1833 a plant nursery was in existence at Ogle's Grove, Hillsborough, adjacent but on the opposite side of the road from the distillery, owned by Hercules Bradshaw, and Culcavy Cottage. In 1910 a house, Ogles Grove, close to the nursery, is recorded as belonging to J. Nicholson R. Pim, who was a director of the Hillsborough Linen Co., Ltd. The Ogles Grove Nursery continued nearby to the house but owned by Joseph Bell.

The photograph shows a gathering of people outside Ogles Grove, an Edwardian villa, in the early years of the twentieth century. Ogles Grove, built *c* 1900, was a two-storey, brick-built house with hipped roof, and windows, sashed, silled and topped with a rounded arch in a contrasting brick. A string course ran level with, and incorporated, the sills of the second storey windows. Ogles Grove was demolished in the 1980s, clearing the grounds for a small development of high quality detached houses.

RAVARNET
HOUSE

Ravarnet House

JFR

IN THE SECOND HALF OF THE EIGHTEENTH CENTURY Ravarnet House belonged to James Henderson, who was a linen draper and possibly a bleacher. Ravarnet House, built in 1789 and latterly greatly extended, is situated approximately one and a half miles south-east of Lisburn, on the Carnbane Road. The building has a rambling informal design and is all two-storey integrating a series of fashionable remodellings including some Arts and Crafts detail from early in the twentieth century. The *Ordnance Survey Memoirs* record that there was a corn mill and a flax mill at Ravarnet in 1834 belonging to John Henderson. Henry Hart purchased Ravarnet House together with 57 acres of land from the Hendersons in 1854. He also took over a flour mill and in adjacent rooms installed a set of looms for linen weaving which laid the basis of a linen weaving business in Ravarnet village. Sir Robert Hart, who became known for his work in the British Foreign Office in China, was the son of Henry and Ann Hart and spent his childhood years at Ravarnet House.

The Hart family occupied Ravarnet House for 18 years from 1855 to 1873 when it was taken over by Mr John Sinton, a member of the well known Sinton family of Tandragee. The Ravarnette Factory was operated by John Sinton & Co. and some years later the concern worked under the title Ravarnette Weaving Co., Ltd, run by Mr Edwin Sinton, son of the previous owner. The factory closed down as a power loom concern after the first World War, in the early 1920s. Edwin Sinton is recorded as living at Ravarnet House in 1909 and he married Olive, daughter of John Pringle, of Clones. The Sintons left Ravarnet House in the late 1920s.

Thomas Sinton began manufacturing linen at Laurelvale near Tandragee in the 1850s where, according to Bassett's *Directory*, by 1887 nearly 700 were employed in the weaving factory. In 1871 Thomas Sinton purchased the Tandragee Flax Spinning Company when it went into liquidation and this mill prospered, the records showing 600 in employment in 1887. Yarns were then spun for the heavy end of the trade at Tandragee but in 1885 Thomas Sinton bought a mill at Killyleagh, Co. Down which made yarns of a very fine grade and 500 were employed in the mill. Thomas Sinton died in 1887 and the business was carried on by his sons Messrs Maynard, Arthur, Thomas and Frederick Sinton. Meanwhile John Sinton, a brother of Thomas, had bought the

Mrs Sinton in the front seat with a group of First World War nurses at Ravernet House

Private Collection

Ravarnette Weaving Factory in 1873 and it also prospered. In 1905 the business was made into a Limited Company, the title being Thomas Sinton & Co., Ltd. The Tandragee mill continued to produce linen yarn into the 1990s but has now ceased production.

Edwin Sinton formerly of Ravarnet House, centre, with on his left F.B. Sinton (Banford House) and on his right Thomas Sinton (Laurelvale) in 1928

Private Collection

3
LISBURN

Market Square, Lisburn

J.H. Burgess

Reproduced with the kind permission of the Irish Linen Centre – Lisburn Museum

THE BARBOURS
OF HILDEN

FROM VERY EARLY TIMES the Barbour family was settled in the Parish of Kilbarchan in Renfrewshire, Scotland and Barbours are known to have held public offices in that district from as early as the year 1496. From Kilbarchan sprang the Barbours of Bolesworth Castle in Cheshire, and their relatives who live in Perthshire, and from Paisley the Barbours of Hilden, Lisburn, in Northern Ireland. Like many of the lairds in Renfrew, Ayrshire and adjoining counties they were engaged in the linen industry and in 1739 they erected a hand loom linen factory near Paisley. The date at which the Barbours added thread manufacture to their linen trade is unknown although by 1783 they are reputed to have been in the trade for some time. Prior to 1783, the Barbours, having experienced the unreliability of Scottish yarns, had been importing Irish yarns to twist into thread in Scotland and John Barbour of Kilbarchan had been attending Irish markets to buy yarns for the firm's requirements.

In 1783 John Barbour leased a property a mile south-east of Lisburn, where he established a thread industry by building a village called The Plantation.

Individual workers' houses were built including a twisting room and nearby there was a bleaching plant and warehouse for packing and despatching. The workers had to be trained but by 1786 the industry was in full production and was known as Barbour's Linen Thread. John Barbour maintained his connection with Scotland subscribing handsomely to charities in Paisley. His success during his career of forty years at The Plantation may be gauged by the fact that his assets were valued at over £60,000 when he died in 1823.

John Barbour's two sons, John (1796–1831) and William (1797–1875) carried on their father's trade but did not see eye to eye. John wanted to continue on conservative lines, but William had wider ambitions in the way of twisting thread by power driven machinery, and the brothers therefore separated. John retained his father's works at The Plantation and William leased the De La Cherois's bleach green of 33 or 34 acres at Hilden in 1824 where he erected a water mill to twist the thread by machinery. Unfortunately John Barbour of The Plantation died in 1831 when still a young man, and William purchased the goodwill and assets, consolidating the business at Hilden. The first modest mill established at Hilden in 1824 was soon replaced by others and, under William Barbour and his sons, the business rapidly developed. Branches were set up in the United States of America at Paterson, New Jersey in 1863, and in Europe, until by 1875 the premises at Hilden had grown to very extensive dimensions, and William Barbour was enjoying outstanding success in his enterprise.

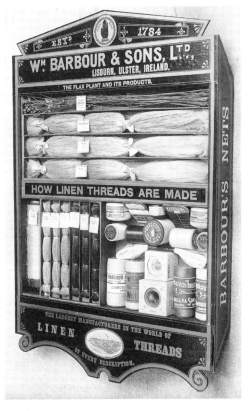

Barbour showcase

William Barbour married Eliza Kennedy in 1821 and had a family of thirteen, eleven of whom married and established for the next generation an extensive cousinship. They had a large family of seven sons and six daughters, no fewer than five of these sons being men of conspicuous business ability. The availability of these young men in combination with the technical innovations in the trade ensured a rapid expansion of the business, with branches in Europe and the United States of America. Three of the sons of William Barbour of Hilden moved to the United States, making their homes there, the first being Thomas Barbour, who moved to New York in 1849 and began thread manufacture in Paterson, New Jersey in 1864, founding the linen thread industry in the USA. Robert Barbour, second son of William Barbour, after living at The Fort, Lisburn went to America in 1864 to manage the first Barbour mill and settled in Paterson, New Jersey. William James Barbour practised for some time as a doctor in the Co. Antrim Infirmary, Lisburn, and later went to America, settling in the town of Quincy, Illinois. Bassett, writing in 1888, states that William Barbour & Sons, Ltd, were entitled to be ranked as the largest manufacturers in the world of tailors' thread and shoemakers' thread for hand and machine sewing. Altogether the company employed over 5,000 people and they took an active interest in their social well being, building houses and schools at Hilden.

The firm was carried on after the death in 1875 of William Barbour by his sons, Messrs. John D. Barbour, DL, JP, Robert Barbour, Samuel Barbour and Thomas Barbour. His eldest son John Doherty Barbour (1824–1901) succeeded his father as Chairman and Managing Director of William Barbour & Sons, and in the thirty years that he occupied that position he did much to advance not only the prosperity of the business, but the welfare of Lisburn and the surrounding district. William Barbour's youngest daughter Maria Pirrie (b. 1843) married Robert Gordon of the firm Gordon & Co., Flax Spinners and Linen Manufacturers and lived at the family home at Hilden. They had two sons, Malcolm Gordon of Clonmore, Lisburn, Director of the Linen Thread Co., Ltd, and of William Barbour & Sons, Ltd, and William Gordon of Hilden House, Director of William Barbour & Sons.

However, the crowning achievement of John Doherty Barbour was the formation of the Linen Thread Co., Ltd, in 1898 when he brought together the Irish, Scottish and American Barbour Companies. The firms which first combined in the Linen Thread Co., Ltd, were:

Wm. Barbour & Sons, Ltd, Hilden
The Barbour Flax Spinning Co., Paterson, New Jersey
The Barbour Brothers of New York
The Marshall Thread Co. of Newark, New Jersey
Finlayson Bousfield & Co., Ltd of Johnstone, Scotland
and of North Grafton, Massachusetts

and later:

W. & J. Knox, Ltd of Kilbirnie
Ainsworth & Co. of Cleator Moor
Dunbar McMaster & Co., Ltd of Gilford and of Greenwich, New York
Crawford Brothers of Beith, Ayrshire
F.W. Hayes & Co., Ltd of Banbridge

In later years the Linen Thread Co., Ltd purchased the firms of Robert Stewart & Sons, Ltd of Lisburn and Lindsay Thompson & Co., Ltd of Belfast, these firms having risen to great prominence in the Irish linen thread trade. The

Linen Thread Co., Ltd expanded worldwide and became the world's largest linen thread producers.

The Right Hon. Sir J. Milne Barbour, DL, MP (1868–1951), eldest surviving son of John Doherty Barbour, was created a Baronet in 1943 having held many public offices in Northern Ireland and having served as a Minister in the Northern Ireland Parliament for eighteen years. Milne Barbour entered the business in 1888 and was responsible for the development of their interests in netting which was sold for the salmon fishing on the western coast of USA and Canada. This was a trade which was to become a significant part of the work at Hilden and Milne Barbour took a considerable interest in it, often visiting Vancouver, British Columbia on sales visits. He was destined to spend sixty-three years in the Barbour business. Sir Milne Barbour succeeded his father and became Chairman and Managing Director of The Linen Thread Co., Ltd and William Barbour & Sons, Ltd in 1905. He was a member of the Northern Ireland Parliament from 1922 until his death serving as Minister for Commerce for sixteen of those years. At his memorial service held in St Anne's Cathedral, Belfast, he was described thus:

> As a captain of industry, he had combined outstanding ability in business with a wide humanity and a graciousness which marked him out as a leader to whom men turned instinctively for guidance and inspiration.

The Prince of Wales (later Edward VIII) visited Hilden Mill on 18 November 1932. He is seen here being escorted by John Milne Barbour (left) and Malcolm Gordon, his cousin, a director of the Linen Thread Company and manager of Barbour's Hilden and Dunmurry mills.
Private Collection

After his death on 5 October, 1951, two of the existing Directors took the chairs of the Linen Thread Co., Ltd and William Barbour & Sons, Ltd for a very short time but eventually one of the Directors, Mr Luke, was appointed Chairman. Over the next twenty years the business diversified to meet the decrease in demand for linen but eventually in 1978 the company was taken over by Hanson. However, the former Barbour works at Hilden still export to over 135 countries, continuing two centuries of thread manufacture.

BARBOUR FAMILY TREE

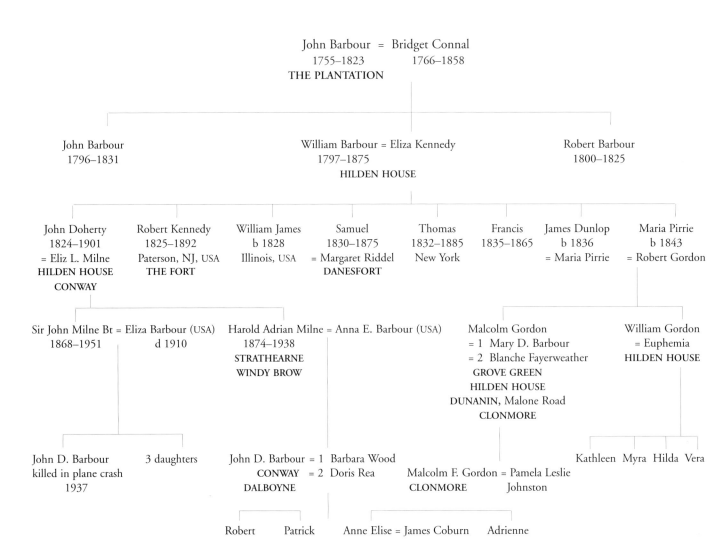

John Barbour = Bridget Connal
1755–1823   1766–1858
THE PLANTATION

John Barbour
1796–1831

William Barbour = Eliza Kennedy
1797–1875
HILDEN HOUSE

Robert Barbour
1800–1825

John Doherty
1824–1901
= Eliz L. Milne
HILDEN HOUSE
CONWAY

Robert Kennedy
1825–1892
Paterson, NJ, USA
THE FORT

William James
b 1828
Illinois, USA

Samuel
1830–1875
= Margaret Riddel
DANESFORT

Thomas
1832–1885
New York

Francis
1835–1865

James Dunlop
b 1836
= Maria Pirrie

Maria Pirrie
b 1843
= Robert Gordon

Sir John Milne Bt = Eliza Barbour (USA)
1868–1951   d 1910

Harold Adrian Milne = Anna E. Barbour (USA)
1874–1938
STRATHEARNE
WINDY BROW

Malcolm Gordon
= 1 Mary D. Barbour
= 2 Blanche Fayerweather
GROVE GREEN
HILDEN HOUSE
DUNANIN, Malone Road
CLONMORE

William Gordon
= Euphemia
HILDEN HOUSE

John D. Barbour
killed in plane crash
1937

3 daughters

John D. Barbour = 1 Barbara Wood
CONWAY   = 2 Doris Rea
DALBOYNE

Malcolm F. Gordon = Pamela Leslie
CLONMORE   Johnston

Kathleen Myra Hilda Vera

Robert   Patrick

Anne Elise = James Coburn   Adrienne

PLANTATION HOUSE
LISBURN

PLANTATION HOUSE was built by John Barbour in 1784 when he set up his linen thread making business in the country close to Lisburn in County Down. This was a large three-bay, three-storied house, with eight bedrooms, in which the top floor housed the Barbour's personal servants, the house also having a basement. The house was roughcast with slated roof and chimney stacks at the gable ends. Adjoining the property was a lower roofed dwelling which was the residence of the mill manager. On the land behind Plantation House there were three flat meadows suitable for bleaching greens and also behind the original house was the complex of buildings known as the factory where linen thread was manufactured. The business flourished and John Barbour lived for thirty-nine years at Plantation House, until he died in 1823. He was succeeded by his two eldest sons John and William, John continuing to run the Plantation and

Plantation House
ILC & LM

living there but William being more ambitious and setting up his own thread mill at Hilden. John Barbour, junior, died in 1831 at the early age of thirty-five but his second wife and their children continued to live at Plantation House until the mid-nineteenth century.

By 1863 Plantation House had passed to a William Kelsey who appears to have made some alterations to the property, notably the bay windows shown on the ground floor. A gate lodge was also erected but it has since been demolished.

HILDEN HOUSE

HILDEN HOUSE is situated about one mile north-east of Lisburn and close to the River Lagan. In 1837 Thomas Fagan in the *Ordnance Survey Memoirs* describes the house as very commodious, a square building, two storeys high and slated. The house, dating from 1824, is an example of Irish Georgian architecture, the walls grey painted roughcast, five bays wide, with hipped slated roof. Hilden House had many improvements over the years during the Barbour family period, notably on the outside, a Victorian veranda type porch, which has since been removed. Originally there was water to hand with a pump and a water engine for watering the garden, which contained about two acres, being enclosed by a stone and lime wall about twelve feet high and well stocked with fruit trees.

Hilden was formerly the site of an extensive bleach green established by Samuel De La Cherois, one of the French Huguenots who assisted in the development of the linen industry in the area around Lisburn. It was his own residence for many years but the entire building had fallen into decay; William Barbour knocked it down and built a new Hilden House when he bought the

Hilden House, built by William Barbour in 1823

ILC & LM

47

William Barbour
1797–1875

ILC & LM

bleach green. According to the records of Market Square Presbyterian Church, Lisburn, William Barbour took up residence at Hilden about the middle of 1824 having married Eliza Kennedy, eldest daughter of Samuel Kennedy of Lisburn, in 1821. They lived first at Bridge End, moving on to Castle Street, Lisburn and finally taking up residence at Hilden in 1824 where they brought up their large family. Eliza Barbour died in 1873 and William aged 77 years in 1875. Hilden House was then occupied by their youngest daughter Maria Pirrie who had married Robert Gordon, and it was subsequently occupied first by their elder son Malcolm and latterly by his brother William who were both involved in William Barbour & Sons, Ltd.

Hilden House has now passed out of the Barbour family and is privately occupied while the rear premises, stables etc. have been converted into the Hilden Brewery.

Hilden House, 2002

JFR

GROVE GREEN
HOUSE

IN 1836 GROVE GREEN HOUSE was described as standing north-east of Lisburn, about half a mile from the town, handsomely situated on the banks of the Lagan, and was built as a cottage, partly thatched and partly slated, standing one storey high. There was a good fruit and vegetable garden; overall the demesne consisted of about forty acres of good arable land divided into fields and there were handsome iron gates to the different entrances. This was the seat of Samuel Kennedy who owned extensive flour mills, locally called the Lisburn flour mills, standing four storeys high and using water wheels to grind the wheat and finish the flour. The Kennedys appear to have been a very old family around Lisburn with records stretching back to the seventeenth century, and living in Lisburn town until 1820 when they appear to have moved to Grove Green. Samuel Kennedy's eldest daughter Eliza married William Barbour in 1821 and

Grove Green House
ILC & LM

by 1824 they were living near to her old home in Hilden House.

In more recent times Malcolm F. Gordon (junior), great-grandson of William Barbour and Eliza Kennedy was brought up as a young child in Grove Green House which, he states, was a small Barbour house, not now in existence, on the Low Road from Hilden to Lisburn. His father, Malcolm Gordon (senior), was persuaded to move into Hilden House as it was convenient to the mill but, in fact, he found it too close to the mill and persuaded his brother Willie to move into Hilden House while he moved out to Belfast.

THE FORT
LISBURN

ROBERT BARBOUR (1825–1892), second son of William Barbour, had this house and a gate lodge built about 1860 near to the Belfast Road into Lisburn. The house was of a substantial stuccoed neo-classical design and later had work carried out on it by Sir Alfred Waterhouse. The front porch shows a great similarity to that of Hilden House.

Robert Barbour went to America in 1864 to join his younger brothers Thomas and Samuel in Paterson, New Jersey where his thread manufacturing knowledge was required in the setting up and management of mills which supplied thread to the Barbours' growing business in the United States. In 1870 he married Sarah Rebecca Edwards and they stayed at The Fort on their occasional visits to Lisburn. In later years The Fort was used as a residence for visitors to the Barbour family, since Robert spent the remainder of his life in Paterson, New Jersey.

Latterly the house was not used by the Barbours, and after the Northern Ireland Education Act of 1948 set out a requirement for secondary education for all children, the house was demolished and the new Fort Hill Girls' County Intermediate School built on the site.

Robert Barbour married Sarah Rebecca Edwards in 1870 and is seen here seated with her outside 'The Fort' where they stayed on occasional return visits to Lisburn.
ILC & LM

CONWAY, DUNMURRY

Conway

BT

CONWAY, one of the largest of the linen houses in the area, was situated on the south side of the old main Belfast to Lisburn Road south of Dunmurry at Derriaghy. In 1852 William Charley of Seymour Hill gave some land from the Seymour Hill estate to his younger brother Edward (1827–1868), to build a house for his first wife Mary (née Caldecott) (1834–1854) from Essex. Edward named the house Conway after the local landowner the Marquess of Hertford, one of whose titles was Lord Conway. Bence-Jones describes Conway as a 'two storey Victorian house with a symmetrical front of two shallow curved bows and a central projection; on either side of which runs a pillared and ballustraded veranda, joining at one end to a single-storey wing, and at the other to a pilastered conservatory. Roof on bracket cornice, Italianate tower.' The architect is not known. At one time there was the Charley crest over the front door.

In 1892 Conway was sold by the Charley family to John D. Barbour of Hilden, who lived there until 1901. The property has two gate lodges, one at the Lisburn Road entrance dating from *c* 1870 and a second at the River Road

The rear of Conway, the dining
room and the drawing room
Private Collection

53

John D. Barbour, DL, JP,
1824–1901. He is wearing the
uniform of the Deputy
Lieutenant for County Antrim.

ILC & LM

Milne Barbour brought this
totem pole back from British
Columbia and erected it in the
grounds of Conway

JFR

entrance which was designed by Henry Hobart. It would appear likely that John D. Barbour commissioned work on Conway by Henry Hobart at a similar time. Certainly the house was very large, having below-stairs apartments and a drawing room which, a member of the Barbour family claimed, was larger than the Throne Room in Buckingham Palace. A description of the house in the 1930s states that it was then a perfect capsule of Victorian/Edwardian taste, with American overtones, like central heating and all the bedrooms being 'en suite'. The great drawing room ran the width of the house and had red velvet curtains swagged with heavy gold braid, with more curtains which could divide the room in two. In the hall and stairway there was dark mahogany panelling, and there were suits of armour, weapons and ornaments. Lovely gardens surrounded the house and there was a cricket ground, putting green and a large swimming pool beside the tennis courts. The estate also had a home farm with stabling for many horses which was of considerable use in World Wars I and II.

John D. Barbour JP, DL was the father of Sir Milne Barbour DL, MP, later Deputy Prime Minister of Northern Ireland, and also Chairman of the Linen Thread Co., Ltd, and he moved to Conway after his father's death. Milne Barbour married his American cousin Eliza, eldest daughter of Robert Barbour, of Paterson, New Jersey, USA, but she died in 1910 leaving a son, John D. Barbour and three daughters. Unfortunately John Barbour was killed in a plane crash in 1935 when trying out a new plane; he had an airstrip at Conway and,

Rt. Hon. Sir John Milne
Barbour, DL, MP,.1868–1951
Painting by Cowan Dobson
ILC & LM

soon after taking off, crashed. Sir Milne Barbour lived in great style at Conway, having twenty-five gardeners and outside staff along with seventeen inside staff. Although he also owned a number of Rolls Royce cars which he used on official occasions, his daily habit was to walk to Barbour's, Hilden from Conway along the River Lagan tow path at the back of Conway. The Linen Thread Co. made salmon nets which were extensively sold in British Columbia and Sir Milne after a business trip there in 1935 brought back a totem pole which he had erected on the front lawn of Conway. Sir Milne Barbour lived in Conway for almost fifty years until he died there in 1951.

Latterly Conway became a Forte Posthouse Hotel and in the 1970s suffered bomb damage but was repaired and remained as a hotel until 1999. The house has now been demolished.

DANESFORT

Danesfort

JFR

Porte cochère, Danesfort, designed by William Barre for Samuel Barbour, 1864

JFR

DANESFORT, MALONE ROAD, Belfast was designed in 1864 by William J. Barre for Samuel Barbour (1830–1875) and was originally known as Clanwilliam House but the name was changed in the 1870s. The house has been described as one of the finest High Victorian mansions in Ireland and is now William Barre's most ambitious extant private house. Built of fine ashlar stonework, Danesfort has features of Italian, French and English styles all rolled into one richly moulded and sculpturesque building. The most imposing feature is the mansard-roofed square tower over the porte cochère which is linked back to the main house by a dramatically expressed service staircase and double height entrance hall. In contrast the principal reception rooms are simply expressed, with the drawing room marked by a colonnaded bow and the master bedroom overhead continuing this bow with coupled colonettes. There is a good arcaded and balustraded stairway in the entrance hall and fine rooms are grouped around it.

Samuel Barbour, fourth son of William Barbour and Eliza Kennedy, was a member of the Board of William Barbour & Sons, Ltd and was driven in his carriage each day from Belfast to Hilden. After his death Danesfort was left to his widow in trust for their daughter who married Charles Duffin in 1883 and it remained in the Duffin family until the 1940s when the house was bought by Gallaher Ltd who then sold it to the Electricity Board for Northern Ireland.

STRATHEARNE HOUSE

STRATHEARNE is situated on the road from Belfast to Lisburn between Finaghy and Dunmurry and has been a girls' school since 1945 when it was renamed Colinmore, as part of Princess Gardens School which subsequently became Hunterhouse College when it amalgamated with Ashleigh House school in 1987. During the Second World War the house, owned by the Barbour family, was requisitioned for war work by Harland & Wolff who built three very large drawing offices at the back of the property. Early in 1945 the Barbours indicated to the Governors of Princess Gardens School that they were willing to sell Strathearne and an agreement was reached that the school should purchase the house and the twelve acre grounds for £18,550 along with the purchase of the three drawing offices from Harland & Wolff for the sum of £2,500.

The original house was built for Philip Fletcher Richardson between 1872 and 1874 on land leased from John Stouppe Charley of Finaghy House. However, in 1876 the house was acquired by Charles Finlay and the name 'Strathearne' appears in the *Belfast & Ulster Directory* of 1877. By 1884 James Macauley is listed as residing at Strathearne, but in 1888, when property in the estate of Mary

Oblique view of the front of Strathearne House showing entrance with porte cochère
Private Collection

Rear view of Strathearne
Private Collection

The inner hall
Private Collection

Stewart Charley, widow of John Stouppe Charley, was for sale in five lots 'the house and lands of Strathairn' were included, the house being described as 'large and substantial and in good repair'.

The drawing room
Private Collection

The lounge
Private Collection

Harold Adrian Milne Barbour (1874–1938), third surviving son of John Doherty Barbour, acquired Strathearne in 1906 and lived there in considerable style with his American wife Anna E. Barbour. The property was considerably revamped and enlarged, perhaps by the architect Vincent Craig, comprising house, offices, garage, chauffeur's house, gate lodge, workman's house, laundry and yard. According to Malcolm F. Gordon, whose father was a first cousin of Harold Barbour, Mrs Harold Barbour took a great interest in houses and ensured that in Strathearne they had all the luxuries of life with a friendly atmosphere and no pomposity.

CLONMORE HOUSE
LAMBEG

CLONMORE HOUSE was situated a short distance north of Lisburn on Harmony Hill and was owned by Lisburn Borough Council, being used as an Arts Centre. Lisburn Rural Council bought Clonmore House and twelve acres of grounds in 1955 with the possibility of use for council offices.

The house, stables and gate lodge were built for James Stewart Reade, a Belfast flax merchant, who commissioned Vincent Craig as architect and is seen in the photograph discussing the plans. The building, which was commenced on a green field site in September 1907 and completed in March 1908, is shown in photographs taken 29th April 1908. The site for the house was acquired by J.S. Reade from his cousin, Minnie Johnson Smyth, who lived at Ingram. Clonmore was built in classic Arts and Crafts style with rendered walls, wide tripartite square paned windows and hipped roof which rises to three banded chimneys. Two tennis courts were laid out at the side of the house. J.S. Reade died in December 1934 and his widow sold the property in 1935.

The Reades were followed in Clonmore by Mr Malcolm Gordon, a Director of the Linen Thread Co., Ltd, and his wife Mrs Blanche Fayerweather Gordon who was an American. The grounds of Clonmore were kept immaculate during

the Gordons' residence with plantings of trees, shrubs, flower beds along with a greenhouse for the production of soft fruit. The Gordons employed a gardener and a chauffeur, who latterly were able to recall a lifestyle in which nobility and gentry were regular visitors for tea parties and social functions at the house.

Clonmore House
ECA

In time, their son Malcolm F. Gordon, also a Director of the Linen Thread Company, and his family, occupied Clonmore until it was finally sold to Lisburn Council in 1955. Malcolm F. Gordon, who was in charge of the technical side of the Barbour business, was also Chairman of the Linen Industry Research Association at Lambeg for a considerable number of years. For many years Clonmore was used as the Arts Centre for Lisburn, but at one period it was part of the Lisburn District Council Offices.

Lisburn Borough Council, having built new Council Offices at The Island, Lisburn, vacated Clonmore in 2000. However, later in the same year the house was destroyed by fire.

Mr Malcolm Gordon (senior) with his wife, Blanche, and his grandchildren in their garden at Clonmore House
Private Collection

STRAWBERRY HILL

STRAWBERRY HILL, a mid-eighteenth century cottage type dwelling, lay about a mile out of Lisburn, along the Ballynahinch Road, on the County Down side of the River Lagan. This pleasant country home, in grounds of twenty-eight acres, sat on a hill overlooking the town with gently rising lawns in front of the house and farm buildings behind the house. In 1785, Strawberry Hill was purchased by the Rev. Andrew Craig (1754–1833), Presbyterian minister in Lisburn, from William Whitla. Although Mrs Craig died in 1807 after bearing six children, the Craig family continued to live at Strawberry Hill. In 1814 Margaret Craig, the eldest daughter, married James Ward of Lisburn, who was linked to the Coulson family. James Ward had firstly married Eliza Fulton of Lisburn in 1803 but she died in 1805 leaving a son Thomas born in 1804.

By far the most famous damask manufacturer in Ulster was William Coulson, born in 1739, whose family lived in Lisburn and like many of its residents were probably connected to the linen trade. Hugh McCall in his book, *Ireland and her Staple Manufactures*, states:

> William Coulson, the founder of the Lisburn Damask Factory, commenced work with a small number of looms, which he erected in a large building convenient to the County Down bridge in that town, about the commencement of 1764. Two years afterwards he raised, on a site granted by the Earl of Hertford, the factory which has since become so celebrated.

William Coulson developed a business which became the first successful vertically integrated one in Ireland. He bought flax, much of it from Derry and the north of Antrim, and supervised the spinning and dressing of the yarn since only the finest could be used in the weaving of damask. The Coulsons bleached their own damask in a field near the factory until 1823, when a bleachworks was erected at Sprucefield on the Ravarnet river.

When William Coulson commenced weaving damask the patterns were primitive but he soon effected an improvement by means of the draw-loom which had draw-boys to raise the warp threads arranged for forming the pattern, and in time even further improvements were made. The industry was essentially a luxury one, producing table linen and the like, decorated with armorial designs, national emblems and heraldic designs. Since he was one of the first manufacturers to be successful in this field he enjoyed a large share of Court favour and the recognition of his success by British royalty added largely to his fame. William Coulson died in 1801 but the manufacture of damask was carried on by John, William, and Walter Coulson who were honoured in 1810 by receiving a Royal Warrant for the manufacture of table linen.

Sometime between the years 1834 and 1837 two firms were created, William Coulson & Sons and James Coulson & Company, and they occupied different parts of the original factory, also allocating various of the properties between the two firms. However James Coulson continued to receive a large share of the orders for the Royal Household and he also received appointments to the holders of the Vice-Regal office at Dublin Castle, the Czar Alexander II of Russia, George I, King of the Hellenes, Leopold, Duke of Tuscany, military messes and from London hotels. These all contributed to make a well known and established business in Lisburn.

At the Great Exhibition in 1851 James Coulson received a diploma and a gold medal but he died in the same year aged seventy-six, leaving his business and all his property to Mr James Ward, Strawberry Hill, Lisburn. However, he also died and Thomas Ward, son of Eliza Fulton and James Ward, became the senior partner in James Coulson & Company, living in Cherry Hill, Malone Road, Belfast.

The second Ward family continued to occupy Strawberry Hill and in 1888 Bassett records a Captain James Ward, JP, son of James Ward and Margaret Craig, in the house. James Ward, who retained a share in Coulsons, resided principally in London, but paid occasional visits to the factory. He was largely instrumental in the formation of the London Irish Rifles, and was its first commanding officer, attaining the rank of Colonel in the Territorial Force. James Ward, CB, BL, JP, died in London in 1897. After a short interval, Coulson's business, including the London premises in Pall Mall, was sold to Messrs Hampton & Sons, Ltd, London. As the linen trade decreased following World War II Coulsons was eventually closed down in 1968, although only after weaving a final pale pink damask tablecloth and napkins for Queen Elizabeth II.

Strawberry Hill was demolished in 1968 after every effort had been made to save it. The house is mentioned in Mary Cummings, *Letters Home to Lisburn, from America 1811–1815.*

68, BOW STREET
LISBURN

ROBERT STEWART learnt the linen thread trade with the Barbours, and on the death of John Barbour (2) of The Plantation in 1831, he commenced manufacturing thread in Lisburn by the hand process. In 1836 he erected his first spinning and twisting mill and by 1845 the firm had become Robert Stewart & Sons when he took his two sons Robert and James Andrew into partnership. Robert Stewart, senior, died in 1858, and his son Robert, junior, in 1882, when James Andrew carried on as sole proprietor.

By 1888 the old mill had become out of date and a new mill was completed in 1889 which produced not only enough yarn for the firm's extensive thread trade, but a considerable surplus of yarn for the open market for weaving into cloth. Unfortunately about 1896 there was a down swing in the linen trade and yarn stocks accumulated but the mills kept up full production. By 1897 yarn stocks all over the trade had risen to large proportions, and prices fell rapidly. The banks wanted more cover in yarns to secure the bills, and James Andrew Stewart brought in all his remaining stocks to the merchants but prices fell catastrophically and he was unable to pull through. Stewart was then an old man and the mill and goodwill were purchased by the Linen Thread Co., Ltd.

The Stewart house was at 68 Bow Street, Lisburn and still exists to-day occupied by W.G. Maginess & Son, Solicitors. Although probably originally standing alone, the house is now part of a terrace and is shown on the Hertford map of 1833, appearing in the 1862 valuation in the ownership of the Stewart family. The building is five-bay, three-storey, the walls cream painted stucco, with slated roof and two sets of chimney pots. The windows are Georgian glazed, 6-over-6-pane sashes throughout and a doorcase framed by reeded columns and a shallow fanlight.

The Stewart house in 2002. The carriage entrance remains as in the earlier photograph opposite

JFR

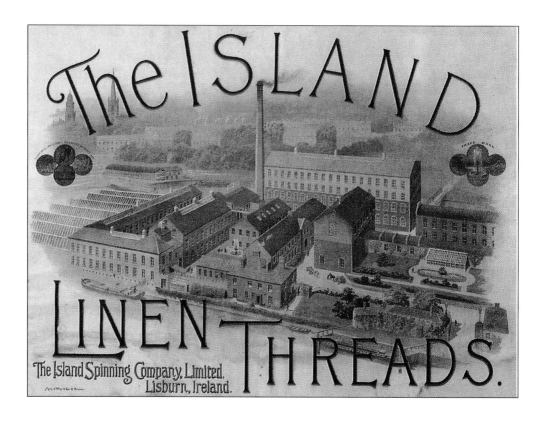

THE CLARKES OF
THE ISLAND SPINNING CO., LTD

THE ISLAND, LISBURN, contains between two and three acres and is formed between the canal and the river Lagan on the eastern side of the town. The land was leased about 1700 by the Marquis of Hertford to the chaplain of the Huguenot settlement but by 1775 it had reverted to the estate. However in 1776 Lord Hertford leased the Island to Messrs Thomas Gregg and Waddell Cunningham of Belfast who started the manufacture of vitriol (sulphuric acid) and other chemicals required for the numerous bleach greens in the neighbourhood, which gave rise to the name Vitriol Island. The premises changed ownership several times and included Dr Crawford, a renowned chemist who lived at Roseville. About 1830 Vitriol Island belonged to Messrs John McCance and William John Handcock who were both involved elsewhere in the bleaching of linen.

A flax spinning mill was built on the Island in 1840 by Mr Samuel Richardson but he died in 1847 and was succeeded by his brother Mr J.J. Richardson, who greatly enlarged the mill. The Island Spinning Co., Ltd, was established in 1867, the premises having been purchased from Mr J.J. Richardson, and the company, in 1871, added an extensive weaving factory. In 1882 the company started the production of linen threads of all kinds for hand and machine sewing, which was of high quality and was exported to America and Europe. The Chairman of the Island Spinning Co., Ltd, was Mr Joseph Richardson (1821–1906) of Richardson Bros. & Co., Belfast, who lived at Springfield, Magheragall. The Richardson family retained a large proportion of the shares in the company which employed in the late nineteenth century about 1,100 workers. Mr George H. Clarke, JP (1840–1923), whose family had been linen merchants in Belfast, was Managing Director and he lived adjacent to the mill at Roseville. After his death in 1923 his son, Edward Stanley Clarke (1879–1960), who had been an assistant manager at the Island Spinning Co., succeeded his father as Managing Director and remained in that capacity until he retired in 1952. Mr E.S. Clarke and his family, who held a minority share holding in the company, lived at Ballyaughlis Lodge, Drumbo, Lisburn.

ROSEVILLE HOUSE
LISBURN

Roseville House
Private Colleection

ROSEVILLE was a Regency villa situated close to the River Lagan on the north-east side of Lisburn and thought to have been built about 1780. The house was on the opposite side of the road from the old Lisburn burial ground of Kilrush and it is recorded as being set in grounds of five acres. Roseville was a two-storey, five-bay house with slated hipped roof and sash windows and according to an advertisement in the *Belfast News Letter*, January 1876 for its letting, contained three reception rooms, five bedrooms and was surrounded by gardens with fruit trees also having the advantage of spring water in the grounds.

The interior of the house on the ground floor was notable in that the drawing room and dining room had fine mouldings in the ornamentation of the ceilings with oval and circular panels. A sloping frieze is also shown in the plan of these ground floor rooms and this had mouldings of circular loops of vine stem with

A section of moulding from
Roseville House
Private Colleection

grape bunches and leaves. A survey carried out on Roseville in 1947 by John Seeds, architect, 7 Donegall Square West, Belfast, states that the plaster work was possibly done by James McCullough, Plasterer of Dublin, who worked between 1761 and 1795.

These front reception rooms at Roseville were also notable for their old French wallpaper. In writing concerning 'Old Wallpapers in Ireland', Mrs H.G. Leask states:

> Of all the 'luxury' types ever available surely none have been more spectacular than the French 'scenic' papers of the first half of the nineteenth century.

The famous series entitled, 'Les Sauvages du Mer du Sud', illustrating the adventures and death of Captain Cook, was represented at Roseville House, Lisburn, by a selection of the full complement of 20 strips. This selection belonged to one of the earliest of the real series of scenic papers, i.e. without a repeat, and as such is very interesting. It was designed by the artist Charvet and first produced by Joseph Dufour at Mâcon, in 1806, before he went to Paris. Plate 1 shows one of the best preserved portions from Roseville, now in the Ulster Museum. This depicts King O'Too near a banana tree and the dance of the O'Tahiti girls which was installed in the drawing room. Another of Dufour's coloured sets, depicting a highly imaginative panorama of the 'Banks of the Bosphorous' and known to have been first issued in 25 strips in 1815, is represented by certain pieces which were in the dining room at Roseville House (Plate 2). Dufour was one of the most successful French wallpaper makers and, as some of his old account books still exist, it is possible to trace most of his output fairly exactly.

Plan of part of the ground floor indicating position of plaster work in principal rooms.
Seeds Collection, MBR

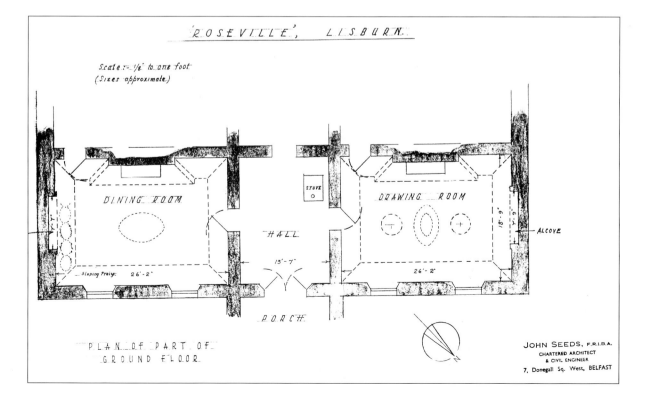

Plate 1:
Captain Cook
Private Collection

Roseville was originally built about 1780 for Dr Alexander Crawford, a physician of eminence, who made vitriol, now known as sulphuric acid, at the Island Chemical Works and this was used in the bleaching of linen. In 1810 the property was occupied by Mr and Mrs Charles Casement and they are reported to have expended a considerable sum of money on general improvements over the next twenty years. This would suggest that it was possibly the Casements who installed the French wallpaper and Mrs Casement continued to live in the house, after her husband's death, until 1840. In the same year a flax spinning mill was built on Vitriol Island by Mr Samuel Richardson and by 1867 the Island Flax

Plate 2:
Banks of the Bosphorus
Private Collection

Spinning Company was established. An extensive weaving factory was added and expansion took place into the production of linen thread in 1882. The Chairman of the Company was Mr Joseph Richardson of Springfield and the Managing Director, Mr George H. Clarke, JP, who lived at Roseville until his death in 1923. His granddaughter, Mrs Rachel Torrens-Spence, recalls the lovely Georgian house which had a large walled garden and yard. She also remembers a walking bridge over the River Lagan from the Island Mill across to Roseville and a bridge for lorries over the Canal to the mill.

Mr George Clarke was succeeded as Managing Director by his son Mr Edward

George H. Clarke, JP, chairman and managing director of the Island Spinning Company, Ltd, at the left of the doorway of Roseville House, following a luncheon on 10 September 1903 on the occasion of a visit to Lisburn by Field Marshall Lord Roberts (second right), commander in chief of the British army during the South African War.

LHS Collection
ILC & LM

S. Clarke who with his wife and family lived firstly at Drumbo Lodge, Pinehill Road, Drumbo and in 1926 moved to Ballyaughlis Lodge, Drumbo. Latterly, Roseville House was owned by the Island Spinning Co., Ltd, and was occupied by Mr Dale who was the last manager of the Company in the 1950s. Correspondence dating from 1945–46 shows that Mr Stendall, Director of Belfast Museum and Art Gallery (now Ulster Museum) and Ada K. Longfield, expert on old wallpapers in Ireland, made some effort to persuade the Island Spinning Co., Ltd, owners of Roseville, to allow the steaming off of the Dufour wallpaper. Photographs were taken of the wallpaper *in situ* in Roseville. However, Mr E.S. Clarke stated that the company wished to carry out alterations in the house, did not wish to sell, and did not want any publicity in case they would be pressurised into handing it over to the National Trust. All that the Museum has from the saved wallpaper is four fragments of the Cook wallpaper and eight fragments from the Banks of the Bosporous; it is not known what happened to the rest of it.

Henry Campbell & Co., Ltd, took over the Island Spinning Company in 1956 and Roseville was sold to the Northern Ireland Housing Trust who divided it into flats. Old cypress trees were felled and the gardens which were notable and had been cared for by Mr Dale became a wilderness. Eventually the Northern Ireland Housing Trust demolished Roseville in the late 1960s and a considerable number of small new houses were erected in the grounds.

Coved cornice
Private Collection

BALLYAUGHLIS LODGE, DRUMBO

Ballyaughlis Lodge
JFR

BALLYAUGHLIS LODGE was previously known as Belvedere Cottage, having been built as part of the neighbouring Belvedere estate circa 1780 which borders the Ballylesson Road close to Ballyaughlis cross roads, and situated between Belfast and Lisburn. This is a one and a half storey slated dwelling, symmetrically planned, Georgian in style with contemporary interiors; the return and stable block are placed around a cobbled open court with coach entrance at the rear. The original building was described in the 1861 valuation as 'a neat double cottage, good style', but small additions were made about 1884 by W.R. Watters. However, in more recent times, when the house was placed on the market in 1990, the accommodation was described as four plus reception rooms, five bedrooms, two bathrooms together with a self-contained granny/teenagers apartment, and double garage. The grounds extended to eight acres with two paddocks and also had an all weather tennis court and an all weather outdoor riding arena.

Belvedere Cottage had many owners prior to Edward S. Clarke, who appears to have firstly rented the property from Durham Dunlop about 1926, when the

name was changed to Ballyaughlis Lodge. At this time E.S. Clarke became Managing Director of the Island Spinning Mill, Lisburn, in succession to his father, and later purchased the house which remained in Clarke ownership until 1982 when his younger daughter, Mary B. Clarke, died. Ballyaughlis Lodge was sold and remains in private ownership.

Edward S. Clarke
Private Collection

The Georgian doorway to Ballyaughlis Lodge

JFR

THE EWARTS OF BELFAST
FORMERLY OF HILLSBOROUGH

William Ewart (1), 1759–1851,
came to Belfast from Annahilt
about 1790. Artist unknown
Private Collection

THOMAS EWART was granted the lease of a farm of twenty acres in the town-land of Carnreagh, Annahilt, near Hillsborough, in 1716. At that time the Linen Board was assisting farmers to procure handlooms of the most modern design and the weaving of damask spread, particularly from Lisburn to Hillsborough and Waringstown. In 1746 the Carnreagh lease was renewed to another Thomas Ewart and in the following generation, in 1759, William Ewart (1) was born. Under his leadership the firm grew from parochial to one of world-wide connections. The Ewarts at first bought locally spun yarns from the cot-tagers around Hillsborough and distributed them to the neighbouring cottage weavers, the resulting cloth being sold to the bleachers.

However, William Ewart (1) had ambitions beyond those of his father and grandfather and about 1790 he moved to Ballymacarrett, then a country village well outside the town of Belfast, where female labour was plentiful. He installed looms and taught the people how to weave linen, purchasing yarn in the sur-rounding yarn markets. Later he began to finish and sell his own cloth. During this period William Ewart kept in touch with Hillsborough and for many years sent a van there every week to collect cloth. With developing sales he appointed agents in various cross-channel centres, his proximity to Belfast facilitating the shipping of his goods. By 1814 William Ewart (1) (1759–1851) had taken his eldest son, William (2) (1789–1873) into partnership, and the firm of William Ewart & Son was established with a town office and warehouse in Rosemary Street.

William Ewart (2) developed the firm into one with world wide connections, bought and perfected bleach works, built and bought spinning mills, weaving factories and warehouses in order to meet the requirements of an ever growing trade. About the year 1840 the firm secured the extensive ground, with water rights, on the Crumlin Road, Belfast, where they built their first spinning mill and in 1850 a power loom weaving factory was added. In 1852 the firm purchased the bleach works at Glenbank, Ligoniel from Mackey and Charters and William (2) went to live at Glenbank House, later moving to Sydenham Park where he died. William Ewart (3) (1817–1889) was taken into partnership in 1843, so that for some years the partners were father, son and grandson.

Towards the end of the eighteenth century a bleachgreen was established at Glenbank, Ligoniel, near Belfast, by the Sinclairs, who remained there until about 1840, when it was purchased by the firm of Mackey & Charters. Subsequently the Glenbank bleachgreen was acquired by the Ewarts in 1852 and by them greatly enlarged and refitted with new machinery. However, there was also a house on the site from the establishment of the bleachgreen. Glenbank House was home to three generations of the Ewart family, the last being Lavens Matthew Ewart, JP, who enlarged the property and built a gate lodge. In 1920, G. Herbert Ewart, then a director of William Ewart & Sons Ltd, offered Belfast Corporation the 'house and grounds of about 7 1/2 acres' known as Glenbank House, for use as a public park. The house was then demolished but the bleach-works continued on the adjoining site until the company closed in 1973.

William Ewart (3) became one of the outstanding figures in Belfast, marrying in 1840 Isabella Kelso, daughter of Lavens Mathewson of Newtownstewart,

Glenbank House, Belfast, adjacent to Ewart bleach works

NMGNI UM

77

Co. Tyrone and had a family of nine sons and five daughters. He was Mayor of Belfast in 1859 and 1860, and also represented the city in Parliament at Westminster from 1878 to 1889, being created a baronet in 1887. The firm enjoyed large sales during the boom years which the linen trade experienced during the American Civil War (1861–1865), the profits made being devoted to the permanent consolidation of William Ewart & Son. In 1883 Sir William Ewart turned his firm into a Limited Liability Company, with a capital of £500,000. The first directors were Sir William Ewart and his five sons who were:

1 Sir William Quartus, DL, MA, (1844–1919) who succeeded his father in 1889

2 Lavens Mathewson (1845–1918) of Glenbank House, Ligoniel – an Alderman of Belfast and a distinguished antiquary

3 Richard Hooker (1848–1918) went as a young man to the American branch of the firm in New York

4 James Mathewson (1854–1898) joined his brother Richard in the firm in New York

5 George Herbert, MA, (1857–1924) of Firmount, Belfast. He was a prominent churchman and worked in the interests of the Forster Green Hospital and of the Maternity Hospital

6 Frederick William, MA, DL, (1858–1934) Barrister-at-law, of Derryvolgie, Lisburn. He was for many years a District Inspector of the Royal Irish Constabulary.

In the twentieth century Ewarts was one of the largest manufacturers and exporters of Irish linen in the western world. Recognition of this was given on

Visit of
Her Majesty the Queen
and His Royal Highness
the Duke of Edinburgh to
William Ewart & Son Ltd
Belfast

8 August 1961
The Queen is welcomed by the chairman, Mr V.F. Clarendon, CBE, DL. The Duke of Edinburgh is shaking hands with Sir Ivan Ewart, Bt, DSC, director.

Belfast Telegraph

8th August 1961, when, on her visit to Northern Ireland, Her Majesty Queen Elizabeth, with His Royal Highness the Duke of Edinburgh, toured the warehouse of William Ewart & Son Ltd, Belfast.

The linen trade worldwide decreased very substantially in the late 1960s and early 1970s with the result that Ewarts came to an agreement with Vantona, an English textile manufacturer, for the takeover of the Company in 1973 and a joint operation with Liddells of Donaghcloney, also owned by Vantona. Many members of the family were recruited into the firm but the last to head Ewarts was Sir W. Ivan C. Ewart, a great-grandson of Sir William, the first Baronet, and the eighth generation from Thomas Ewart of Carnreagh.

EWART FAMILY TREE

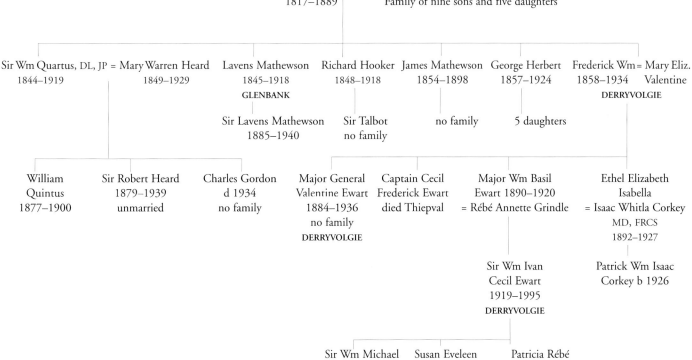

Thomas Ewart – lease of land at Carnreagh 1716

Thomas Ewart – lease of land at Carnreagh 1746

William Ewart (1)
1759–1851

William Ewart (2) **GLENBANK**
1759–1873

Sir William Ewart (3) = Isabella Kelso Mathewson
1817–1889 Family of nine sons and five daughters

Sir Wm Quartus, DL, JP = Mary Warren Heard	Lavens Mathewson	Richard Hooker	James Mathewson	George Herbert	Frederick Wm = Mary Eliz.
1844–1919 1849–1929	1845–1918 **GLENBANK**	1848–1918	1854–1898	1857–1924	1858–1934 Valentine **DERRYVOLGIE**
	Sir Lavens Mathewson 1885–1940	Sir Talbot no family	no family	5 daughters	

William Quintus 1877–1900

Sir Robert Heard 1879–1939 unmarried

Charles Gordon d 1934 no family

Major General Valentine Ewart 1884–1936 no family **DERRYVOLGIE**

Captain Cecil Frederick Ewart died Thiepval

Major Wm Basil Ewart 1890–1920 = Rébé Annette Grindle

Ethel Elizabeth Isabella = Isaac Whitla Corkey MD, FRCS 1892–1927

Sir Wm Ivan Cecil Ewart 1919–1995 **DERRYVOLGIE**

Patrick Wm Isaac Corkey b 1926

Sir Wm Michael   Susan Eveleen   Patricia Rébé

DERRYVOLGIE HOUSE

DERRYVOLGIE was built about 1835 by Mr William Gregg, one of Lord Hertford's agents, in a demesne of twelve English acres with extensive plantations of trees on the northern outskirts of Lisburn. The house is situated on an elevated site and was originally surrounded by extensive gardens, which have gone, but mature shelter trees remain. This square two-storey house with an eaved slated roof and an iron veranda was added to a cottage said to date from the early 18th century or late 17th century.

In 1898 Derryvolgie was bought from the Gregg family by Mr Frederick William Ewart, son of Sir William Ewart, 1st Baronet. At this time Derryvolgie was enlarged, a wing being added with a three sided bow surmounted by a half-timbered gable. Interior alterations were also made, a large hall was formed by making an arch between the staircase hall, which contains a curving staircase,

Curving staircase at Derryvolgie seen through the arch between the main hall and the staircase hall

JFR

Frederick Ewart
Private Collection

and the adjoining room. Both rooms were given fretted ceilings while the drawing room was given a frieze of Georgian style plaster work and an Adam Revival chimney piece set under an inglenook arch.

F.W. Ewart was educated at Wadham College, Oxford becoming a barrister-at-law, called to the Bar, King's Inn, Dublin, 1888. However, he was for many years a District Inspector of the Royal Irish Constabulary, but finally he became Managing Director of the family linen firm, William Ewart & Son, Ltd. After the death of Mr F.W. Ewart, MA, DL, in 1934 Derryvolgie passed to his eldest son, Major G.V. Ewart and on his death in 1936 the house was rented to his daughter Eileen Cotton and her husband. Subsequently Derryvolgie was inherited by a grandson of Fred Ewart, Sir Ivan Ewart, 6th Bt who lived there from the 1950s until 1970. During the late 1960s a fire caused extensive damage to the house and initiated the selling of the property to the Ministry of Defence, who occupied it until 1978. The Water Service purchased Derryvolgie House in 1979 and rebuilt the north wing in a similar style to the rest of the house, continuing to use the house for business purposes to the present day.

Frederick William Ewart and his grandchildren, including Ivan Ewart, seated at left
Private Collection

The river Lagan

Hans Iten

From a Private Collection

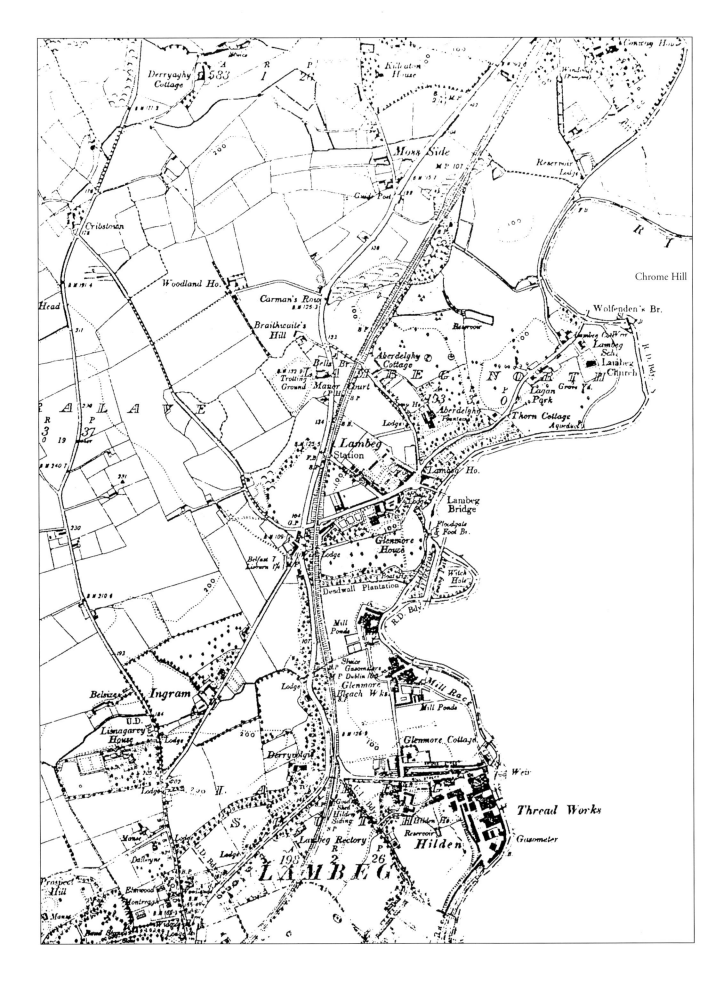

Chrome Hill

4

LAMBEG

Lambeg House
Drawn by Joseph Molloy, engraved by E.K. Proctor, 1832
Reproduced with the kind permission of the Linen Hall Library

THE RICHARDSONS OF LISBURN, LAMBEG AND BESSBROOK

Richardson linen stamp
NMGNI UM

THE RICHARDSONS ARE UNDOUBTEDLY one of the oldest of the linen families, who, generation after generation, pursued the making and marketing of linen. The name is purely English in origin and the Richardsons appear to have been among settlers who were encouraged to come over, chiefly from the West of England and Wales, to live in Lisnagarvey, the modern Lisburn. Sir Fulke Conway had a grant of a vast estate centring around Lisnagarvey which was laid out about 1610, containing fifty-two houses, and among the householders were Steven Richardson, Symon Richardson and John Ap Richard. Almost contemporary with these early settlers was the Rev. John Richardson, rector of Loughgall, Co. Armagh whose brother Zachary also settled in Loughgall and had a son Jonathan Richardson (1) who became a member of the Society of Friends in company with the Nicholsons of Co. Armagh, the Greers of Co. Tyrone, the Grubbs of Co. Tipperary, and perhaps later the Hoggs and Handcocks of Lisburn. The Society of Friends discouraged marriages outside their religion and the Richardson family observed this rule for many generations, the first Jonathan's grandson Jonathan (2) (1681–1737) marrying Elizabeth Nicholson. His son John (1719–1759) served his time to the linen trade with his relatives the Hoggs of Lisburn and he settled there permanently having married Ruth, daughter of William Hogg, who had a bleach green at Glenmore, Lambeg.

The family lived in Castle Street, Lisburn where their son Jonathan (3) was born in 1756 and he in turn was also involved in the linen industry buying, some time prior to 1800, the Hunters' bleach green at Glenmore. Bleaching of linen could only be carried out in the summer months, at that time, and Jonathan was the first to succeed in winter bleaching which meant he was able to run his bleach works all the year round. The business increased substantially and about 1830 the firm purchased the adjoining bleach green from the Handcocks, and amalgamated it with their existing works. Jonathan Richardson (3) and Sarah Nicholson had three sons, James Nicholson (1), John and Joseph, who were to lay the basis for the large Richardson linen business.

James Nicholson Richardson (1) (1782–1847) married in 1810 Anna Grubb of Anner Mills near Clonmel, Co. Tipperary, a lady who brought him a large amount of money. Under his active guidance the Richardson linen business

Jonathan Richardson of Glenmore, 1811–1869

ILC & LM

prospered and in 1825 he took into partnership John Owden, founding the company of J.N. Richardson, Sons & Owden, Ltd, although at that time his sons were not of age. However, as his sons reached maturity, James gradually left the management of the business to Mr Owden and his own elder sons, especially the second, John Grubb Richardson. James Nicholson Richardson lived until 1847, having purchased Lambeg House and renamed it Glenmore in 1835, but had relinquished active direction of the business some time before his death. He left seven sons, some of them becoming men of distinction in the linen trade:

Jonathan (5) (1811–1869) of Glenmore, Lambeg
John Grubb, (1813–1890) of Brookhill, Lisburn; Moyallon and the Wood House, Bessbrook
James Nicholson (2) (1815–1899) of Lissue
Joshua Pim (1816–1882) of Cheltenham
Thomas (b. 1818) of New York
Joseph (1821–1906) of Springfield, Magheragall, Lisburn
William (1824–1862) of Brooklands, Belfast.

The eldest son Jonathan (5) although retaining his financial interest in the family business, cultivated the life of a country gentleman at Glenmore, rather than that of a merchant prince. The strict rules of the Society of Friends did not appeal to him and he became an enthusiastic member of the Church of Ireland, belonging to the Parish of Lambeg. His son, Charles H. Richardson of Cedarhurst, Belfast, was for some years chairman of Richardson, Sons & Owden, Ltd until his death in 1931.

John Grubb Richardson, the second son, was in many ways the most remarkable of the seven brothers since as a young man he showed such unbounded energy in the business that, under the guidance of John Owden, he was gradually installed as the responsible head of the rapidly increasing business. In a brief autobiography he states:

> From 1838 to 1841 I was much occupied with settling my younger brothers in business. It was my great desire that the seven brothers should be bound together and help one another through life.

He was successful in this and in 1838 he assisted his brothers James Nicholson (2) and Joseph to found, along with himself, the firm of Richardson Brothers & Co., of Belfast. In 1840 this firm opened an office in Liverpool for the import of flax, grain and various types of raw material from abroad and the export of linen yarn and cloth. They became associated with the Inmans in the shipping business in Liverpool and with them established the once famous line of steamers, The Inman Line. This entailed the opening of the American firm of Richardson Watson & Co. of Philadelphia and New York about 1846 and Thomas Richardson, the fifth brother, was its head. However, in 1854 the Richardsons fell out with the Inmans on a matter of conscience and sold out their interest, although Thomas remained in New York acting for Richardson Sons & Owden and eventually again for the Inman Line.

Joseph Richardson returned to Belfast about 1856 as head of the firm of Richardson Bros & Co. of Belfast, also becoming Chairman of the Edenderry Spinning Co., the Island Spinning Co. and Richardson's Chemical Manure Co. He died at his home Springfield, Magheragall, Lisburn in 1906.

In 1846 John Grubb Richardson purchased from Lord Charlemont the Mount Caulfield estate in Co. Armagh where his cousins the Nicholsons had been in the linen trade for generations. He built there the nucleus of the model village of Bessbrook with large spinning mills, Bessbrook Spinning Co., Ltd, which were extended later by the addition of weaving factories, all working in conjunction with the Glenmore Bleach Works and the Belfast warehouse of Richardson Sons & Owden. John Grubb Richardson firstly married Helena Grubb of Cahir Abbey, Co. Tipperary, by whom he had one son James Nicholson (3) who became Chairman of the Company and died in 1921 without issue. Some time after the death of Helena he married Jane Marion Wakefield of Moyallon by whom he had one son T. Wakefield Richardson and seven daughters, the sixth of whom, Edith, married her cousin, R.H. Stephens Richardson, DL, who in time became the Chairman of Richardson Sons & Owden, Ltd, and the Bessbrook Spinning Co., Ltd.

The third brother James Nicholson (2) after the separation from the Inmans, left Liverpool and settled at Lissue, Lisburn; he was a partner in the firm of Richardson Brothers & Co., of Belfast. The next brother Joshua, being delicate in early life, apparently took no part in the business, and lived firstly at Aberdelghy, Lambeg and secondly in Cheltenham, England. The fifth brother Thomas settled in America where his descendants still live. The sixth brother Joseph was involved in the firm of Richardson Bros & Co. of Belfast, Liverpool and New York eventually returned to Ireland and continued as head of the Belfast firm until his death in 1906. He lived at Springfield, near Lisburn, leaving six sons, the two eldest George Fennel and Robert in conjunction with their cousin J. Theodore Richardson carrying on the firm which latterly was known as Richardson Bros & Larmor, Ltd. The seventh and youngest son William, succeeded his elder brother John Grubb in the active management of the three branches of Richardson Sons & Owden, Ltd, of which he was Chairman and Managing Director for several years before his death in 1862, aged thirty-eight.

RICHARDSON

Jonathan = Elizabeth Nicholson
1681–1851

John = Ruth Hogg (John served his time with
1719–1759   the Hoggs of Lisburn)

Jonathan = Sarah Nicholson (Jonathan lived in Castle Street, Lisburn.
1681–1851   He bought Hunter's Bleach Green, Glenmore)

James Nicholson = Anna Grubb   John = Harriet Greer
1782–1847   1782–1843

Jonathan	John Grubb	Ruth	James Nicholson	Joshua	Thomas	Joseph	William
1811–1869	1813–1890	1814–1876	1815–1899	Pim	b. 1818	1821–1926	1824–1862
GLENMORE	BROOKHILL	ABERDELGHY	LISSUE	1816–1882	New York	SPRINGFIELD	
= Louisa Houghton	= 1 Helena Grubb	Fred Clibborn					
	THE WOODHOUSE						
	MOYALLON						
	= 2 Jane Marion Wakefield						

Charles Herbert
1855–1931
CEDARHURST
= Helen Richardson

John = Emily Black   Alexander Airth = Susan Grubb
1833–1889   1842–1909   1835–1919   1838–1913
LAMBEG HOUSE   ABERDELGHY

Bertha	Robert Airth	Helen	Laura	Nora	Adelaide	Kathleen
1863–1934	= Evelyn Barbour	= C.H. Richardson	= William	1870–1942	= Mulliner	
LAMBEG HOUSE			Richardson	LAMBEG HOUSE	Rigby	

FAMILY TREE

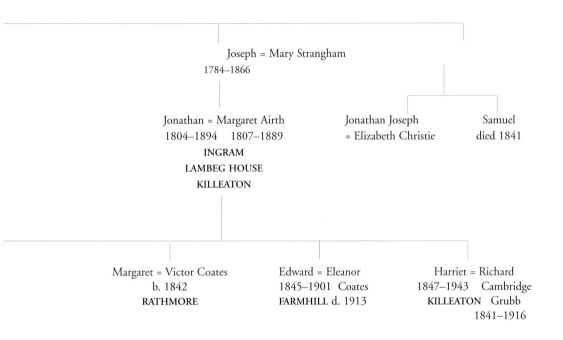

Joseph = Mary Strangham
1784–1866

Jonathan = Margaret Airth
1804–1894   1807–1889
INGRAM
LAMBEG HOUSE
KILLEATON

Jonathan Joseph
= Elizabeth Christie

Samuel
died 1841

Margaret = Victor Coates
b. 1842
RATHMORE

Edward = Eleanor
1845–1901 Coates
FARMHILL d. 1913

Harriet = Richard
1847–1943   Cambridge
KILLEATON Grubb
1841–1916

GLENMORE HOUSE

Glenmore House

ILC & LM

FOR OVER TWO CENTURIES Glenmore House has been one of the most important houses associated with the linen industry in the Lagan Valley. The original property is thought to have been built early in the seventeenth century, and Francis Seymour, Lord Conway, resided there for some years when it was known locally as 'The Lord's House' at the beginning of the eighteenth century. Glenmore House is situated about a mile and a quarter north of Lisburn in the village of Lambeg and adjacent to the old main Belfast to Lisburn Road. Thomas Fagan writing in 1837 in the *Ordnance Survey Memoirs*, described the house as a beautiful, square structure, two storeys high and slated. The front of the house faced south with a boldly projecting portico and tall roof parapet lending neo-classical gravity, with a fine cornice raised round the entire building. At either end of the square house stood handsome round apartments, the same height as the house, and also at both ends of the house stood extensive wings, one storey high. In 1837 the demesne or grounds attached to the house contained between seventy and eighty English acres which were situated on either side of the Lagan river and canal. The garden, about one and a half English acres,

was stocked with a variety of fruit trees and there was a greenhouse, grapery and peach houses, glass-roofed and measuring one hundred and twenty-two feet in length. In front of the house there was a large lawn, interspersed with a variety of forest trees.

The doorway of Glenmore House
JFR

Since 1760 Glenmore House has in turn been the home of several linen families. Firstly, it was purchased in that year by Mr John Williamson who was a linen bleacher, and played a very prominent part in the early development of the linen trade. As well as writing an able treatise on the trade, he was instrumental in having a bye-law passed by the Trustees of the Linen Board in 1762, by which all brown linens had to be sealed so as to certify that each web was of proper length, breadth and workmanship. 'This,' he said, 'would not only save much time to the buyer, but tend to give confidence to consumers and a higher reputation to their national trade'. Although the bye-law was a just one, essential to the reputation of the trade, it was most unpopular with certain sections of the trade, and on the pretext that Williamson was the enemy of the people, three or four hundred weavers assembled in Lisburn and armed with blackthorn sticks marched from Lisburn to Lambeg in search of Williamson. Lord Hillsborough, who was in sympathy with Mr Williamson, rode immediately into Lisburn and placing himself at the head of a body of soldiers set off for Lambeg. Unfortunately, before their arrival, the windows of 'Lambeg House' had been broken and considerable damage done to furniture and the building

LAMBEG HOUSE.

To be SOLD by PUBLIC AUCTION, at Mr. HYNDMAN'S, Belfast, on FRIDAY, the 10th of October inst. at TWO o'clock, P. M.

LAMBEG HOUSE and LANDS, containing about 70 Acres, English Measure, situate within one mile of Lisburn, and six of Belfast, held under the Marquis of Hertford, by Lease for three young lives, all in being, at the Yearly Rent of £1, 1s. per Acre. The House is in good order, and fit for the immediate reception of a large family. The Garden is fully stocked, walled on one side, and contains, with a Greenhouse, a range of Glass of 120 feet in length, with Vines and Peaches in full bearing—the whole of the best construction, and in perfect order.—The Grounds are ornamented with extensive Plantations of old and new Trees and Shrubs, and are beautifully situated on the River Lagan. The Offices are extensive. There are eight Cottages for Labourers, including Porters' Lodges at the extremities of the two approaches from Belfast and Lisburn; and also an Ice House.

For further particulars, apply to R. WILLIAMSON, Esq. Lambeg House; or to DAVID LEGG, Esq. Lisburn and Carrickfergus. (652

Notice of sale of Lambeg House *Belfast News Letter* 7 October 1834. Lambeg House was purchased by Mr James Nicholson Richardson, 1782–1847, and in 1835 was renamed Glenmore

itself. On his retirement from business, Williamson went to live in London but before his death he returned to his home at Lambeg, where he died, and was buried in Lambeg Churchyard, in that part which is known as 'The Nuns' Garden'.

Glenmore staircase before and after restoration
JFR

The original house, up to this time, was not very large but in the late eighteenth century it became the property of Mr John Handcock, who enlarged it considerably and carried out many improvements. In 1811 Mr Handcock's bleach green at Lambeg was broken into but knowing that the penalty was death he refused to prosecute the accused. With the aid of Mr John McCance, of Suffolk, and other linen merchants, Sir Samuel Romilly, MP, was induced to bring in a bill to the House of Commons for the milder punishment of bleach green robbers. Lambeg House was next occupied by Henry Bell, Esq., and then in 1808 by Robert and Alexander Williamson. They were the sons of the earlier owner John Williamson and in 1808 Robert was Honorary Secretary of the Belfast Committee of the Linen Board and subsequently a JP.

In 1835 'Lambeg House' was purchased by Mr James Nicholson Richardson (1782–1847), founder of Richardson Sons & Owden Ltd, and it remained in the Richardson family until 1901. Mr Richardson was responsible for changing the name from 'Lambeg House' to Glenmore House, Glenmore being a name associated with the area in which the house stands, but another possible reason could be the existence of a second Lambeg House which was built by Mr Alexander Williamson about 1785. This was originally known as Lambeg Village House but the name was shortened to Lambeg House and latterly in the twentieth century was known as 'The Chains'. After his purchase of the house in 1835 James Nicholson Richardson employed Thomas Jackson to make extensive improvements c.1840, including a totally new front entrance area, but leaving the older portion of Glenmore at the rear of the building. He also added East and West gate lodges to the two entrances to Glenmore. Jonathan, eldest son of James N. Richardson, inherited Glenmore after his father's death in 1847 and married Lousia Houghton in 1850. Whilst he retained a financial interest in Richardson Sons & Owden, Jonathan preferred the life of a country gentleman and Glenmore was a very important social centre in the 1850s and

1860s. The Richardson family continued to occupy Glenmore House until 1901 when it was purchased by Mr John M. Milliken, who was better known as a coal importer than a linen man. He was very generous in making Christmas gifts of coal to all widows in Lambeg village. During his time of residence at Glenmore House, the estate was the scene of many 12th of July demonstrations when Lambeg drums were in evidence.

In 1919 the Linen Industry Research Association was formed and Glenmore House chosen as a suitable location for research into all aspects of the manufacture of linen, from the propagation of the flax seed to the final processes of the bleaching, dyeing, and finishing of the fabric. Indeed, at this point Glenmore became a focal point for the Irish linen industry. At first only part of the house was required by the Association as laboratories, but as the scope of the research work widened so also did the need for more accommodation until all of the thirty-four rooms and attics were in use either as laboratories, offices or stores. A comprehensive range of outbuildings surrounding the courtyard was also used as technical laboratories and workshops. After the Second World War, when technical innovation became central to the linen industry, the work of the Linen Industry Research Association expanded to include members in Scotland, and enquiries were received from all over the world.

However, in the 1990s, the greatly diminished linen industry could no longer

The West Lodge of Glenmore House built *c* 1840. The architect was Thomas Jackson.
P.J. Rankin

Linen Institute Research Association. Some Council members and senior members of staff at Glenmore, *c* 1972

Private Collection

support the now renamed Lambeg Industry Research Association and it was forced to close. This ended more than two centuries of the association of the linen industry with Glenmore House when the property and grounds were sold to building developers in 1993.

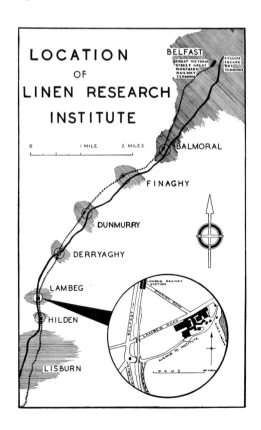

ABERDELGHY

ABERDELGHY, situated close to the village of Lambeg and known then as 'Lambeg Cottage', was built in 1815 by Mr Henry Bell, linen merchant. This was a commodious double house, two stories high and slated, with a considerable return, and set in grounds of forty-eight English acres. The entrance, close to Bell's Lane, Lambeg, was by a handsome winding avenue. According to maps prepared by Thomas Pattison, Lisburn, *c* 1833 Aberdelghy was in the ownership of Joshua Richardson who enlarged the premises and added a gate lodge, in company with his brothers, probably using the architects Thomas J. Duff and Thomas Jackson. However, Joshua Richardson did not enjoy good health and left Ireland for the more temperate climate of Cheltenham and the house, around 1860, became the property of his sister Ruth, young widow of Frederick Clibborn of Moate, and sister of Jonathan Richardson of Glenmore.

Mrs Ruth Clibborn bequeathed Aberdelghy to her cousin Mr Alexander Airth Richardson, who lived there with his wife, Susan Grubb, and family from 1877 until his death in 1919. He made considerable improvements to the property including building a second gate lodge for an entrance to Aberdelghy off Bell's Lane, Lambeg. Bence Jones describes the building as, 'An irregular two storey

Alexander Airth Richardson,
1 December 1905
PRONI

97

house of mid-19th century aspect; shallow gables with bargeboards; hood mouldings over windows.' Alexander Airth Richardson was the son of Jonathan Richardson, MP, of Lambeg House; he was born at Ingram House, Magheralave in 1835 and was in business as a linen manufacturer and bleacher.

In 1920 Aberdelghy was purchased by Mr W.R. McMurray, the then Chairman of the Lambeg Bleaching, Dyeing and Finishing Company. The whole property was finally sold in the late 1950s to Lisburn Borough Council for a golf course and Aberdelghy was demolished.

Aberdelghy House

INGRAM

Ingram House

MBR

INGRAM, MAGHERALAVE, was situated about one mile from Lisburn on the old Belfast Road and was rebuilt in 1828 by Reverend John Corken. The new house was a commodious, five-bay square building two storeys high and slated, with an oblong wing attached to the east side. The house and yards were partially sheltered by trees with shrubberies and gravel walks in front of the house which was set in a demesne of thirty-four acres.

Ingram became the home of Jonathan Richardson (1804–1894) and Margaret Airth about 1830 and they were to remain there for almost twenty years, when they moved to Lambeg House. While there the property was improved, and, in common with his cousins and the fashion of the time, he added a gate lodge to the entrance. Jonathan Richardson was the son of John Richardson and Harriet Greer, succeeding his father as owner of the Lambeg Bleaching, Dyeing & Finishing Co., Ltd.

Ingram continued to be occupied until well into the twentieth century but without connection to the linen industry. The house was demolished circa 1966 and the site developed for new housing.

The staircase and upstairs landing
showing ceiling moulding

MBR

SPRINGFIELD
MAGHERAGALL

SPRINGFIELD is situated about three miles west of Lisburn on the road to Ballinderry and adjacent to Magheragall Parish Church. In 1850 Joseph Richardson married the daughter of Major Richard Rollo Houghton, owner of the original dwelling, and later in 1855, when he had retired from the Richardson business in Liverpool, he acquired the Springfield property and demesne. Thomas Jackson, architect, enjoyed the patronage of the Richardson family having worked at many of their seats such as Glenmore, Old Forge and Lissue. Joseph Richardson engaged Jackson to design a new villa and gate lodge at Springfield and he did both in his recognisable stuccoed neo-classical style. Springfield, one of the last linen houses remaining in private ownership, is a large two-storey house with hipped and slated roof, decorative chimney pots and projecting eaves supported on paired brackets. The walls are smooth rendered with moulded surrounds to the windows which have segmented heads to the first floor and plain sashes. The panelled entrance door is set in an engaged portico with entablature supported on console brackets.

The west front of Springfield
JFR

Joseph Richardson lived at Springfield until his death in 1906 and the house remained in the Richardson family till 1928. The property was then

Joseph Richardson 1821–1906

101

Fergus Wilson 1872–1957

The canted bay at the centre of
the south front of Springfield

JFR

bought by Mr Fergus Wilson (1872–1957), a director of one of the major Irish linen companies, Blackstaff Flax Spinning & Weaving Co., Ltd, who lived there with his sister Miss Leila Wilson. Mr S.N.F. Wilson was a brother-in-law of Mr Thornton Boyd, a great-grandson of one of the founders of Blackstaff, Captain Boyd. In time Fergus Wilson became Chairman of Blackstaff and was one of the well known personalities in the linen industry. Springfield was well maintained by him and he had a chauffeur, Mr McGrain, who lived with his family in one of the gate lodges. A second gate lodge was also occupied and the staff comprised a parlourmaid, a housemaid, cook and a general gardener/handyman. In 1950, after the death of his sister, Fergus Wilson left Springfield moving to Norton, 155 Malone Road, Belfast.

The original Springfield, an eighteenth century cottage, still stands in the grounds and was described in the *Ordnance Survey Memoirs* as a very neat oblong house, slated and standing one storey high. In 1837 Thomas Fagan wrote that the house was originally an ordinary farmhouse but about 1770 Edward Wakefield acquired the property and rebuilt it. Around 1811 Major Houghton got a new lease and subsequently made several improvements to the house and demesne which then consisted of about eighty-seven English acres.

LISSUE

LISSUE is situated about one and a half miles from Lisburn, on the road from the latter to Ballinderry, the house standing on a height commanding views of the surrounding countryside in Counties Antrim and Down. Lissue is a two-storey, with two curved bows on its entrance front, large rather rambling house with extensive out buildings to the rear including accommodation for servants, stables and coach houses. The house has a natural slate hipped roof with lead ridge and hip rolls, it is finished in smooth painted render above an ashlar stone base and topped with a parapet. There is a central recessed entrance with Ionic columns and pilasters behind which is a pair of entrance doors each with three panels decorated with beading. According to the *Ordnance Survey Memoirs* the house was built about 1807 for Robert Garrett, Esq., but in 1830 it was sold to Captain Crawford who improved the house and the demesne.

Lissue House
JFR

After the separation of the Richardson Liverpool business from the Inmans, James Nicholson Richardson (1815–1899) left Liverpool and settled at Lissue, Lisburn which he had enlarged and improved. Richardson commissioned Thomas Jackson *c* 1855 to extend Lissue to the rear and to add East and West Gate Lodges which were built in the neo-classical style. He was a partner in the firm of Richardson Bros & Co., Belfast, who were linen yarn merchants and lived a further forty years at Lissue. Although James N. Richardson died in 1899 the family lived on at Lissue until

James N. Richardson
1815–1899

The side view of Lissue House

JFR

well into the twentieth century. In 1941, during the Second World War, the then owner Colonel Lindsay lent Lissue to the Belfast Hospital for Sick Children as a refuge from air raids, and finally in 1947 gave the house and demesne to the hospital as a gift. The hospital used the house principally as a convalescent home for children up to 1988 but it is now occupied by the Livestock & Meat Marketing Commission for Northern Ireland.

The staircase and landing window

JFR

KILLEATON

KILLEATON, situated between Lisburn and Dunmurry and adjacent to the main road appears to have been built about 1870 for Richard Cambridge Grubb of Cahir who married Harriet Richardson, daughter of Jonathan Richardson, MP, of Lambeg House. The house built in brick, was three-bay, two-storey with a hipped and slated roof, and having a front extension to the right of the building.

Richard C. Grubb joined the Richardson linen business in Belfast. In their later years Jonathan Richardson, MP, and his wife Margaret Airth lived in retirement at Killeaton with their daughter Harriet. Richard Grubb died in 1916, his widow continuing to live on in the house until she was very old. Latterly the land surrounding the house was developed for housing and Killeaton was demolished.

Killeaton House around 1900. The domestic in the doorway was Margaret Maguire, housekeeper at Killeaton House. The young man is almost certainly Richard Grubb (junior) and the older lady, Mrs Grubb (senior).

ILC & LM

LISNAGARVEY HOUSE

Lisnagarvey House
ILC & LM

IN 1855 THOMAS JACKSON, the Belfast architect, was commissioned by Sarah Malcolmson née Richardson for the design of Lisnagarvey House, a villa in a small park with gate lodge, on the Belsize Road, Lisburn. Thomas Jackson had already been commissioned by various members of the Richardson family on extensive improvements to their properties, such as Glenmore at Lambeg and Lissue outside Lisburn. Sarah D. Richardson married David Malcolmson of Clonmel, and they lived for a time at Suirbank, near Clonmel, where the Malcolmsons, members of the Portlaw Quakers, were cotton spinners. After being widowed, she returned to Lisburn, where she built Lisnagarvey, a house much too large for her own needs, but which was a rallying place for her younger brothers and sisters after her eldest brother, Jonathan Richardson, married and occupied Glenmore. Mrs Ruth Clibborn of Aberdelghy, Lambeg, would often come and stay with her elder sister Sarah at Lisnagarvey, Lisburn.

Sarah Malcolmson died in 1864 leaving Lisnagarvey House to her youngest sister, Anna R. Pim, widow of Joshua Pim of The Glen, Whiteabbey, which was a Pim family property. She continued to use the large house, as her sister had, to care for any members of the large Richardson connection who were in need of a helping hand or a listening ear. Anna Pim lived at Lisnagarvey until her death in 1906.

Lisnagarvey House was a pleasant, L-shaped, stuccoed, two-storey, early Victorian building with hipped roof, and triple glazed Georgian windows on the ground floor. The house and its demesne were swept away in 1968 to make way for a housing development.

Anna R. Pim

THE PRIORY
LAMBEG

The Priory, 1961, with a slated
roof, sits on the left of the
photograph. The gate lodge to
Aberdelghy is visible in the
distance. Lambeg House is on
the right hand side.

BNL

The Lambeg date stone, 1676

JFR

LAMBEG VILLAGE is said to have been built in the year 1676, and a stone bearing that date, was later built into a house belonging to Mr Henry Bell, immediately behind his own house, The Priory, according to Rev. H.C. Marshall. This date stone, along with another which reads HENRY BELL LAMBEG 1840, are placed near the eaves of a very old two-storey house, one of a row, to the rear of The Priory. In the eighteenth and nineteenth centuries Lambeg had a square where Lambeg Fairs were held, such as on Easter Monday and Midsummer's Day. Part of this area is still to be seen in the photograph of Lambeg village in 1961 with Lambeg House on the right hand side, and The Priory on the left close to Bell's Lane and the gate lodge of Aberdelghy. The Priory, is a two-storey, five-bay Georgian house, seen in the 1880 photograph with a thatched roof and tall chimney pots. The later 1961 photograph shows a slated roof and the house has been painted white but is otherwise unchanged. This building still remains in Lambeg and is occupied by Mr Thomas Herron.

The name of Henry Bell arises frequently in histories of Lambeg village and one can only assume that grandfather, father and son bore the same name and, indeed, were all in the business of merchanting linen. In *Heterogenea*, published in 1803, we read:

In the Parish of Lambeg is the village of that name, and the houses of Samuel Delacherois, Messrs. Richard, Thomas and Abraham Wolfenden who carry on the manufacturing of cotton, paper and blankets; Lambeg House, now Mr Henry Bell's, linen draper; Mrs Barclay's, Mr Williamson's, etc.

The side view of The Priory showing the thatched roof, 1880

ILC & LM

It must be noted that Lambeg House subsequently became known as Glenmore when in Richardson ownership.

Thomas Fagan, writing in 1837 in the *Ordnance Survey Memoirs* about Lambeg village, had, as his informant, Mr Henry Bell, linen merchant, living in Lambeg Cottage which he had built in 1815 and which later became known as Aberdelghy.

LAMBEG HOUSE

Lambeg House
ILC & LM

JOHN WILLIAMSON who established the Lambeg Bleaching works about 1760 and lived in what was then known as Lambeg House, latterly Glenmore, had two sons Robert and Alexander. They both became involved in the linen industry: Robert was Honorary Secretary of the Belfast Committee of the Linen Trade in 1808. Alexander Williamson built Lambeg Village House about 1785 but in 1837 Thomas Fagan, in the *Ordnance Survey Memoirs*, records the dwelling as 'Lambeg, a Seat', occupied by the Misses Williamson, daughters of the late Alexander Williamson. After 1835, when the former Lambeg House was renamed Glenmore by James N. Richardson, the Williamson house became known as Lambeg House.

The *Ordnance Survey Memoirs* describe the house as a commodious, oblong building, two storeys high and slated, with a good office house attached and set in grounds of twenty-seven English acres. A notable feature was a brass sundial set in the fruit and vegetable garden. This sundial had been made by Edward Spicer of Dublin and purchased by John Barclay who had it erected in Lambeg in 1771. Marshall mentions an enlargement of the house in the early years of the nineteenth century which, in effect, created two houses connected to each other. At this point one house was occupied by Mr David Barclay, a linen bleacher and owner, for a time, of the Lambeg Bleach Works.

In 1849 Lambeg House passed into the ownership of another extensive linen bleacher, Mr Jonathan Richardson, MP, who represented Lisburn in the Imperial Parliament for fifteen years. He had previously lived at Ingram Lodge for twenty years. Lambeg House remained in the Richardson family for around a further hundred years, John Richardson succeeding his father in Lambeg House when his parents moved in retirement to live with their daughter Harriet Grubb at Killeaton. John Richardson (1833–1889) became head of Richardson & Co., Lambeg Bleachworks and a partner with his brother Alexander Airth Richardson and Richard Nevin in building in 1865 Lambeg Weaving Company.

The last members of the family residing in 1933 at Lambeg House were the Misses Bertha M. and Norah Richardson when it was colloquially known as The Chains as a consequence of the chains surrounding the front garden. However, Norah Richardson died in 1942 and subsequently the house had several owners until it eventually became a hotel which was destroyed by a terrorist bomb in 1975.

THE WOLFENDENS OF LAMBEG

The Wolfenden coat of arms

JFR

THE EARLIEST BEARER OF THIS NAME that has been identified here is Abraham Wolfenden. According to Marshall's *The Parish of Lambeg*, the family is of Dutch origin, and apparently, like the Mussens and the Muntzes, was introduced here during the Duke of Ormonde's Lord Lieutenancy in his effort to establish the linen trade in the 1660s. Abraham Wolfenden has no memorial in Lambeg churchyard so we do not know the date of his birth or death; there are tombstones in the Wolfenden enclosure recording the deaths of his descendants for many generations and on these they are described as 'Linen Drapers'. They also established a paper making works where the old Lambeg Weaving Company factory stands between the Ballyskeagh Road and the river Lagan. The Wolfenden's original small farm dwelling, out of which the present Chrome Hill has grown, was probably built sometime during the second half of the seventeenth century, and known then as Lambeg House.

Richard Wolfenden (1723–1775) set up a works to manufacture woollen blankets on the County Antrim side of the river Lagan beside River Road about 1750 and these blankets enjoyed wide popularity in the English and Dublin markets for their superior quality and finish. Thomas Wolfenden had a tuck mill for finishing and shrinking the blankets made by his brother Richard. Richard Wolfenden, who had renamed the house Harmony Hill, died in 1775 and his sons carried on the business. The Wolfendens added the manufacture of calicos and muslins to their business but eventually, about 1825, they moved to Dublin, and became muslin factors at the Linen Hall. The last of the male representatives of the family recorded in Lambeg Churchyard is John who died in

Wolfenden gravestone in
Lambeg Churchyard

JFR

1829, though a Thomas Wolfenden is recorded as being a Churchwarden in Lambeg Parish Church as late as 1886.

In 1783 Anne Jane Wolfenden married John Charley (1744–1812) of Finaghy, who had served his time with Richard Wolfenden of Harmony Hill. It appears, though there is no actual proof, that while Richard's sons carried on the blanket business, the linen business passed to his son-in-law, John Charley, whose sons, John and William eventually transferred it to Seymour Hill in 1822.

Early in the 1830s, the Lambeg Works, by then also producing cotton goods, calico and muslin, were sold to Richard Niven of Manchester who named the house Chrome Hill, to commemorate his discovery of the use of bichromates for the fixing of colours in textile printing. Niven was very successful, his printworks were extensive with two printing houses and many ancillary buildings. In 1844 Jonathan Richardson rented the premises from Richard Niven and, about 1866, Richard Niven Jnr. joined in partnership with John and Alexander Richardson to build a weaving factory alongside the dyeworks. Lambeg Weaving Co., Ltd, Ballyskeagh, continued in business well into the twentieth century.

WOLFENDEN FAMILY TREE

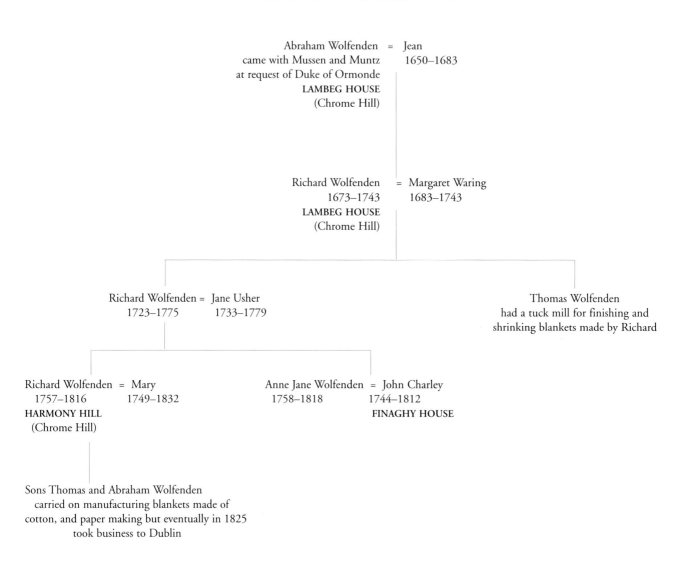

Abraham Wolfenden = Jean
came with Mussen and Muntz 1650–1683
at request of Duke of Ormonde
LAMBEG HOUSE
(Chrome Hill)

Richard Wolfenden = Margaret Waring
1673–1743 1683–1743
LAMBEG HOUSE
(Chrome Hill)

Richard Wolfenden = Jane Usher
1723–1775 1733–1779

Thomas Wolfenden
had a tuck mill for finishing and
shrinking blankets made by Richard

Richard Wolfenden = Mary
1757–1816 1749–1832
HARMONY HILL
(Chrome Hill)

Anne Jane Wolfenden = John Charley
1758–1818 1744–1812
FINAGHY HOUSE

Sons Thomas and Abraham Wolfenden
carried on manufacturing blankets made of
cotton, and paper making but eventually in 1825
took business to Dublin

CHROME HILL
LAMBEG

CHROME HILL, built on a rise of ground overlooking the river Lagan at the Wolfenden Bridge, Lambeg, is situated on the old coach route from Belfast to Lisburn. The original small farm dwelling, known as Lambeg House, out of which the present house has grown, was probably built sometime during the second half of the seventeenth century by Abraham Wolfenden. Indeed, if he was not the builder of Chrome Hill, he is its earliest known occupant since in 1690 he is said to have supplied the timber needed to repair one of King William's wagons, when it broke down at the ford over the Lagan, where the Wolfenden Bridge now stands. The King is said to have waited in Abraham's house while the wagon was being mended.

The present owner of Chrome Hill, well known architect, Robert McKinstry,

Chrome Hill.
The eighteenth-century front seen from the south
Dermott Dunbar

115

Chrome Hill from the south west
Dermott Dunbar

The front doorway
Dermott Dunbar

has recorded a history of the development of the house in the *Lisburn Historical Journal*, Volume 6. Many features in the present house make it clear that Chrome Hill developed from a two-unit, two-storied or lofted house of hearth/lobby formation, with the stairs at the rear of the chimney stack between it and the back wall, a practice commonly seen in English hearth/lobby houses of the seventeenth century, but rarely found in Northern Ireland. Abraham Wolfenden's original seventeenth century house can be sorted from the later additions by looking at the existing ground plan and taking note of the large, very deep chimney breast in the room which has always been the kitchen, immediately to the right as one enters through the front door.

Robert McKinstry states that sometime around the 1760s the original house was heightened, remodelled and extended, by adding a three-storey wing on to the west side, three rooms long. The difference in floor levels between the old and new blocks, and the way they are set at right angles to each other, suggests that this wing may have already existed as a cloth store, positioned close to the house for security, giving the building a T-shaped

116

form. At this time, the front door was moved westwards by three bays, to open into a proper little entrance hall, made out of the front part of the second room in the original house. From here, a fine staircase was built to a spacious landing, which leads into a large sitting room made out of the original loft above the hearth room. McKinstry states that these changes reflected the relatively more sophisticated, formal and even spacious life style of the eighteenth century factory owner which is underlined by the architectural embellishments introduced as part of the improvements and indeed much of this mid-eighteenth century detail still survives intact. A surmise may be made that it was probably the

The drawing room: the principal 18th century room on the first floor

JFR

117

Richard Niven, son of
Richard Niven of Chrome Hill

ILC & LM

The Niven crest set in the
pediment above the door

JFR

second Richard Wolfenden who undertook such an ambitious rebuilding, when at the age of twenty he succeeded his father in 1743. The work may well not have been carried out until after he had married Jane Usher, and renamed the house Harmony Hill.

Further changes to the building were made post-1830 when Richard Niven bought the house, renaming it Chrome Hill, and inserting his own crest in the pediment above the front door. On the west of the house Niven added the wide two-storey elliptical bow and remodelled the dining room inside the bow with arched recesses for sideboard and cupboards. Sometime before the 1860s, Niven made a new main entrance to the house just west of an original secondary steep driveway up to the stable yard and the back of the house. This driveway described a wide semi-circular sweep up to the front door giving the visitor the best view of the west front and made redundant the old driveway which originally ran straight from the house down to the river. In the twenty-first century Niven's new entrance gates and the entrance opposite the factory with its original eighteenth century gates and piers remain in use. Niven died in 1866, but his widow lived on at Chrome Hill until her death in 1899 although in the previous year the house had been purchased by John Milliken, a Belfast coal merchant and property speculator.

Edwardian alterations were probably made by Milliken when he lived for a short time in the house in 1900. The entrance hall was enlarged and a pine sheeted bathroom and cloakroom were made at the same time within the walls of the house. At this time the house was roughcast and the stone quoins which are visible in an old photograph were cut back and cemented over. However, Milliken only lived briefly in Chrome Hill before moving to Glenmore and renting the house firstly to a Major Adam Jenkins and subsequently to Benjamin Hobson, whose family owned the linen works at Ravarnet. In 1921, Milliken sold the house to F.G. Barrett who only stayed three years, selling the building in 1924 to Mrs Downer, who remained in possession of the house for the next forty-three years. After her death in 1967, Chrome Hill came on the market and Robert McKinstry and his wife bought the property and continue to live there.

The walkway from the front door of Chrome Hill overlooking the River Lagan.

Dermott Dunbar

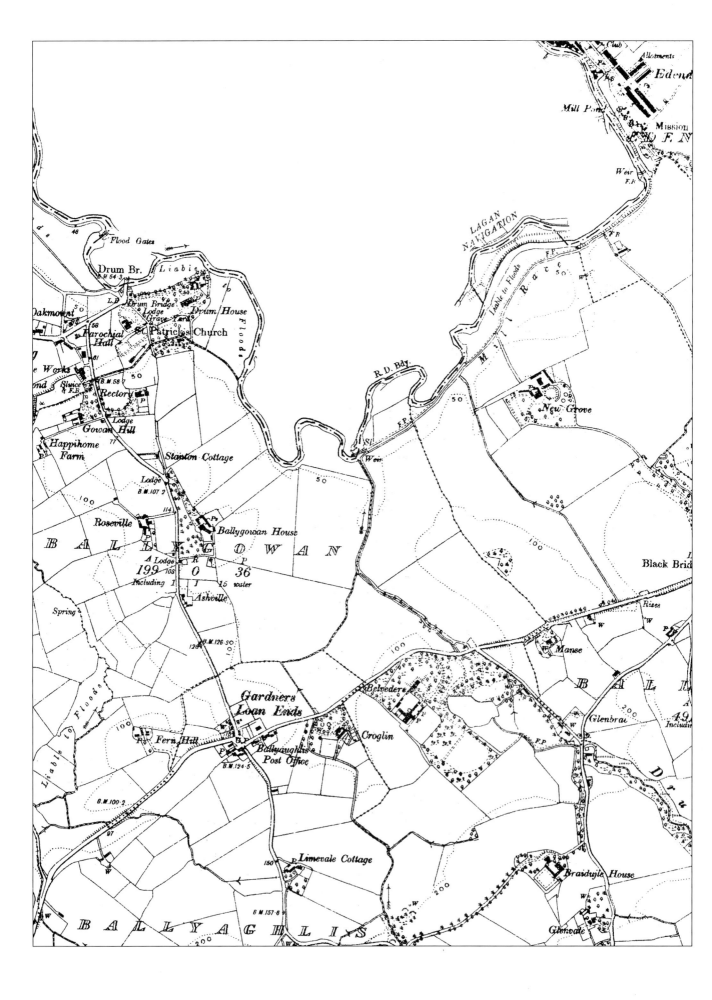

DRUMBEG

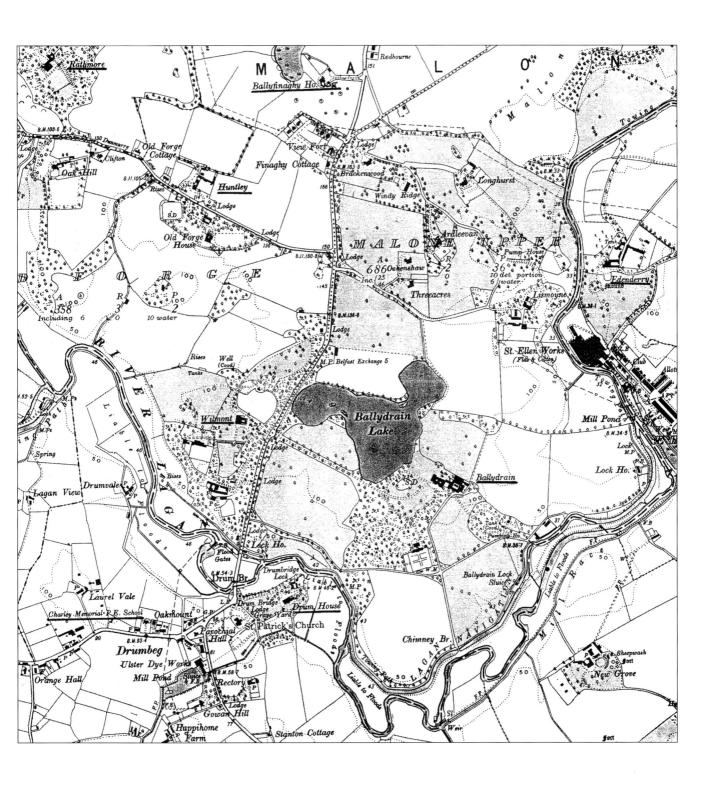

DRUM HOUSE
DRUMBEG

Drum House

JFR

WALTER HARRIS in his *Antient and Present State of the County of Down*, published in 1744, notes that this residence '… the House of James Hamilton Maxwell Esq., stands on a small rising Hill in View of the River, which here runs in Meanders down to Drum Bridge on the Road from Lisburn to Belfast, and the Place is adorned with good Plantations.' In fact the area of countryside near Drum Bridge was dominated by three demesnes situated in close proximity to each other: Wilmont and Ballydrain, seats of the Stewart family and Drum House, home of the Maxwells. The original Drum House was probably built in the late seventeenth century and is illustrated in Joseph Molloy's drawing engraved by E.K. Proctor in *Belfast Scenery in Thirty Views*, published in 1832.

The Maxwell family of Drum House was involved in linen and appear to have founded a bleach green at Drumbeg in the early years of the eighteenth century apparently where there is now housing named The Hermitage on the site of the old Thompson's Dyeworks. By 1725 bleaching had already passed beyond the reach of the ordinary weaver and numerous bleach greens were being set up. In

1725 Hamilton Maxwell of Drumbeg was given a grant of £40 a year for three years by the Linen Trustees as wages for a Dutch bleacher 'who shall bleach after the best manner used at Harlem' on condition that he made a bleachyard and built a bucking house according to the Trustees' specifications. Maxwell was also supposed to have built the first scutch mill in the county about 1747. However, the processes involved in the bleaching of linen were by no means efficient and machinery for finishing was only gradually coming into use. McCall in *Ireland and her Staple Manufactures* states 'Machinery driven by water power for beetling linen was first introduced in 1725 by Mr Hamilton Maxwell of the Drum'. Again McCall states that 'Mr Maxwell's works became very celebrated', and over time beetling was universally adopted by the bleachers and finishers.

Drum House in E.K. Proctor's *Belfast Scenery in Thirty Views*.

The much older rear section of Drum House, possibly 18th century

JFR

After James Hamilton Maxwell's death in 1751 the estate remained in the Maxwell family certainly until 1812 when a Miss Letitia Maxwell, probably his daughter, lived in Drum House, and conveyed the land for the building of Drumbeg Church in 1795. William Hamilton Smyth, owner of Drum House

Drum Bridge, showing the linen beetling mill which would have been driven by a water wheel. A sluice gate can be seen beyond the mill building.

Illustration from the supplement to the *Dublin Penny Journal*, vol. 4, July 1835 – June 1836, showing the old road and bridge over the river Lagan.

in 1836 and a member of the Assizes, placed before the Grand Jury a proposal to establish a new road, which by-passed Drum House and Drumbeg Church. Up until 1837 the road across Drum Bridge swung sharply left before it reached Drumbeg Church and wound along the side of the church grounds, past Drum House demesne. The new road was established, Hamilton Smyth being financially responsible for its upkeep and the old road was closed in 1849.

William Hamilton Smyth continued to occupy the property until 1861 when he was followed by Miss Eleanor Moore, treasurer of the Ragged School, Barrack Street, Belfast until the mid 1860s. The *Belfast News Letter*, 15 October 1873, contains an advertisement for the sale of both mill and house by Mr W. Greenfield, owner of Drum House. In the late 1870s – early 1880s John Arnott Taylor of Arnott & Co., Belfast, drapers and milliners, was the owner of Drum House. He employed Thomas Jackson, architect, to front the old house with a late Victorian stuccoed neo-classical villa, and also repeated the exercise to a

smaller scale on the gate lodge at the main gate. Sir David Taylor purchased Drum House in the spring of 1883 and he was a brother-in-law of John Arnott, the previous owner. The property changed hands a number of times prior to the present owners, Morrell and Mrs McNeice who came to Drum House in 1959 and the grounds, laid out in large gardens, are now known as the Drum House Nurseries.

The present Drum House is stucco painted cream, three-bay, two storeys high and slated, quoins adorn the corners of the front elevation, and the doorway is reached by a small flight of steps. The roof is hipped with moulded eaves and cornice supported on paired console brackets, the sash windows are surrounded by moulded architraves and a string-course separates the first and second storey.

> ALL persons to whom Arthur Hamilton Maxwell, Esq; late of Drumbeg in the county of Down, died indebted, are desired forthwith to send in an account of their several demands and the nature of them whether by bond, bill or otherwise, unto his executrix at Drumbeg aforesaid, in order to have the speediest method taken for their payment; and likewise all persons who were indebted to him are desired to pay off the demands upon them unto his said executrix. Notice is likewise hereby given, that the mansion house with the offices and domaine thereunto belonging, will be set for 17 years, and proposals received by the executrix; the house a good house, with 4 rooms on a floor, very pleasantly situated near the river Laggan, within three miles of Lisburn and four of Belfast; the domaine very good land, well planted, all profitable ground, arable and meadow, consisting of about 100 acres; the garden well planted with fruit trees on the walk and standers, and at present well furnished with all things for the use of the kitchen. The person who shall take the house may have any lesser quantity of the domaine as he shall think most convenient. There is also a large quantity of fir and ash timber to be sold at present.

Notice of letting of Drum House, Drumbeg, after death of Arthur Hamilton Maxwell, Esq.

Belfast News Letter, 12 July 1757

JFR

WILMONT
DUNMURRY

James Bristow's initials on the
wall adjacent to the front door

JFR

THE ORIGINAL WILMONT was built *c* 1760 by William Stewart, son of John Stewart (1701–1784) of Ballydrain; its situation is given in the *Ordnance Survey Memoirs* as three miles north-east of Lisburn and contiguous to the old Malone Road leading from Lisburn to Belfast. The house was described as a commodious structure, two storeys high with a double roof and situated in a demesne of 108 Irish acres, which was planted with forest trees. William Stewart established an extensive bleach green in the grounds but by 1815 this was no longer in use. Wilmont became unoccupied in 1830 after the death of John Stewart, William's son, who died without issue, and by 1837 the house had fallen into a state of disrepair.

The estate was eventually bought by James Bristow, a director of the Northern Banking Company, about 1858 and in 1859 the old house and out buildings were pulled down, although traces of the old Wilmont are still to be seen near the stable block. A new Wilmont, designed by the architect Thomas Jackson, was built and the *Belfast Directory* records show James Bristow in residence in 1860. Bence Jones in a *Guide to Irish Country Houses* describes Wilmont as a plain two-storey Victorian house having a three-bay front with balustraded porch; lower wing ending with tower as high as main block. The upper storey of the main block has segment-headed windows and there is an eaved roof on bracket cornice. Bence Jones also mentions an adjoining front with central curved bow and one bay on either side.

Thomas Jackson designed the building as a double mansion, to house both the family of James Bristow, and that of his son, James Thompson Bristow; the second entrance can be seen on the opposite side of the house to the balustraded porch which has the initials 'J B' on the adjacent wall. The late Lord Glentoran has been quoted as saying the house was 'really only a large semi-detached', since he remembered Sir Thomas Dixon in the 1920s having walls knocked down to unite the two halves into one dwelling. The Park also included interesting outbuildings, previously used in the bleaching of linen, a walled garden, gate lodges, and a lock-keeper's house. James Bristow died in 1866 and his eldest son James Thompson Bristow, also a banker, took over the property. He died at Wilmont in 1877 aged 50 and his trustees sold the estate to Robert Henry Sturrock Reade in 1879.

THE DEMESNE OF WILMONT, AND LANDS adjoining, comprising part of the Townlands of Upper Malone and Dunmurry, in the County of Antrim—one part containing 200A. 3R. 24P., Statute measure, or thereabouts, is held in Fee-Farm, under the Marquis of Donegall, at a rent of £61 0s 2d, besides duties and heriot, subject to an outstanding Lease of 56A. 3R. 20P., for a term of 61 years, from November, 1814, at a yearly rent of £19 9s 6d; and the remainder, containing about 27A. 0R. 1P., Statute measure, or thereabouts, is held by Lease, under the Marquis of Donegall, for a term of 61 years, from May, 1840, at the yearly rent of £8 18s.2d, besides duties and heriot. These Lands are within about four miles of Belfast, and a few minutes' walk of the Dunmurry Station of the Ulster Railway, and are beautifully situated on the banks of the Lagan, and afford a magnificent site for a gentleman's residence, or for villas. The Lands are in prime condition, and have a very desirable aspect. The soil is dry, and capable of producing very early crops. The greater portion of the Lands have been thorough-drained in the best and most effectual manner, and are abundantly supplied with water.

Private proposals will be received up to the 16th of May next, by Messrs. HUGH WALLACE & CO., or the Northern Banking Company, Belfast.

For Rental, Maps, and further information, apply to Messrs. HUGH WALLACE & CO., Solicitors, Downpatrick; 30, North Great George's Street, Dublin; and 70, Victoria Street, Belfast. 1279

Sale of the demesne of Wilmont
Belfast News Letter, 21 May 1856

R.H.S. Reade, JP, DL Chairman and Managing Director of York Street Flax Spinning Co., Ltd.
Private Collection

Directors of York Street Flax Spinning Co., Ltd, July 1908

FRONT ROW: John S. Porter, Sir William Crawford, Vice Chairman, R.H.S. Reade, Chairman, John Mitchell, Sir Thomas J. Dixon, Bart.

BACK ROW: L.E.B. Craig, O.B. Graham, William Chaine, D. Lowson, Secretary, J.S. Reade, J.H. Stirling, J.G. Crawford.

There are many owners of noteworthy houses in this photograph. O.B. Graham of Larchfield, J.S. Reade of Clonmore, Sir William Crawford of Mount Randal, R.H.S. Reade of Wilmont who was followed in Wilmont by Sir Thomas Dixon.

Private Collection

Robert Henry Sturrock Reade, JP, DL (1837–1913), elder son of Dr Thomas Reade of Belfast, was educated at Coleraine Academy, and was apprenticed to York Street Flax Spinning Company in 1854. In 1856 he was sent to New York to organise the firm's business interests in the very large Irish linen market in the USA. Returning to Belfast Reade was appointed a Managing Director of York Street in 1864 and eventually became Chairman of the Board from 1888 until his death in 1913. However his linen interests extended beyond York Street and in 1876 he was elected President of the Linen Merchants Association, and in 1888–1905, President of the Flax Supply Association. R.H.S. Reade, JP, DL, died in 1913 in Dublin, and the property passed to his son George.

In 1919 Wilmont was sold to Sir Thomas and Lady Dixon who entertained lavishly and used it as one of their three residences. Sir Thomas Dixon, who, like R.H.S. Reade, was a member of the Board of the York Street Flax Spinning Co., Ltd, died in 1950. Lady Dixon died in 1964 but a year before her death, 3rd April, 1963, the Wilmont Estate was officially handed over to Belfast Corporation. The house was shortly afterwards opened as a home for old people, but has since had to close, and the grounds were opened to the public, having the name the 'Sir Thomas and Lady Dixon Park'.

During the 1939–45 War, Wilmont was used as an officers' mess for war personnel whose offices were in Ballydrain House. In the 21st century, the extensive grounds and world renowned Rose Garden, established by Belfast City Council at the Sir Thomas and Lady Dixon Park, give great pleasure to the public, while Wilmont is unoccupied but kept in good repair.

Wilmont from the south-east
JFR

Wilmont, Lisburn Lodge, *c* 1880. The gate lodge was built by R.H.S. Reade.
JFR

BALLYDRAIN

Ballydrain, 1918
Hugh Montgomery

THE EARLY HISTORY OF BALLYDRAIN involves the Stewart family of Scottish origin, the first house being built there by William Stewart in 1608 as a fortified farmhouse. This estate is situated on the Upper Malone Road opposite Wilmont, which is now known as the Sir Thomas and Lady Dixon Park. However the Stewart family lived at Ballydrain for over two centuries and in the mid-eighteenth century the house was an L-shaped building situated directly at the head of an avenue of lime trees and on a site which today is a car park. During the eighteenth and the early nineteenth centuries the Stewarts were involved in farming and linen in common with many other landowners in the Lagan Valley, with a number of bleach greens being situated at Ballydrain, Wilmont, Edenderry, Newforge, Dunmurry and Lambeg. In 1834 the Ballydrain estate was sold to Hugh Montgomery, a director of the Northern Banking Co., and he planned a new, more stately house, choosing the eminent English architect Edward Blore for its design.

Hugh Montgomery's house was built *c* 1837 in the Tudor Revival style and of undressed stone, with shouldered gables, mullioned windows and tall chimney stacks as well as a corbelled oriel over the entrance doorway. A gate lodge was also designed by Blore, Belfast Lodge, and built across the avenue from the older Stewart lodge which was demolished. Ballydrain was further enlarged *c* 1876 for Thomas Montgomery to the design of William Henry Lynn, who made a new entrance porch and added a bay window to a garden front. In 1880 a billiard room was added, as well as a conservatory which was erected by James Boyd & Sons of Paisley. A second gate lodge, the Lisburn Lodge, was built in 1880 close to Drum Bridge and on a sloping site. Hugh Wyndham Montgomery sold Ballydrain in 1918 to John Barbour Morrison, a director of the Ulster Spinning

Ballydrain in the late 1860s
Hugh Montgomery

Ballydrain, 1876 after alteration involving the movement of the main door.
Hugh Montgomery

Company, Linfield, Belfast.

Ballydrain was occupied by the Morrison family until 1940 when, like Wilmont, the house was taken over by the Army during World War II, and the Morrisons moved to their property in Donaghadee commuting daily to Linfield Mill by train. In November 1947, on J.B. Morrison's death the Ballydrain estate became the property of his son Maynard Morrison and of J.B. Morrison's brother James. For a number of years the house at Ballydrain was unoccupied, although the land was farmed until the estate was purchased by Malone Golf Club in 1960. The house was reopened in 1962 as Malone Clubhouse and restored but at the expense of its original character. The Tudor chimneys and balustrades were removed, as were the mullioned and transomed windows, and the main entrance was also considerably altered.

The Ulster Spinning Company Ltd was originally set up in 1866 by John Murphy, Adam Duffin and Conway Grimshaw, to include the Linfield Mill, The Charters and the Bath Place Mill, Falls Road, and weaving factories containing about 1,000 looms. Business was good during and immediately after the American Civil War but in the 1890s the shares of the company fell to practically nothing. Early in the twentieth century the company was divided into the Ulster Spinning Company and the Ulster Weaving Company, both with premises on the original Linfield site. The Ulster Spinning Company comprised the

Malone Golf Clubhouse,
formerly Ballydrain
JFR

Linfield Mill and the Grove Mill and was owned by three families, the Morrisons, the Mackies and the Metcalfes.

However, one of the partners, Arthur W. Metcalfe, came to Belfast as a partner of the firm Morrison & Metcalfe, of the Grove Mill, which became a branch of the Ulster Spinning Co., Ltd. In England linen thread manufacture developed on lines similar to those in Scotland and Ireland, indeed flax had been grown in most English counties for domestic use and was chiefly required for the manufacture of sailcloth, tents and fishing nets. All these were cottage industries but about 1790 the first primitive dry spinning mills driven by water power began to be erected in various parts of England, but chiefly in Nidderdale, Yorkshire. John Marshall of Leeds was the pioneer in the development of the machinery and about 1825 he developed machinery for the wet spinning of yarn which was to revolutionise the trade. By 1850 there were about twelve yarn manufacturers in the north of England and these included J. & G. Metcalfe of Pateley Bridge. The Metcalfes, who were long established in Nidderdale as brewers and millers, erected in 1812 the Glasshouse Mills for the spinning of flax on the old dry spinning system. They adapted their plant with the development of wet spinning machinery and gradually changed to spinning yarn for weaving rather than thread twisting, having an extensive trade with all the Yorkshire linen manufacturers. In 1896 the Metcalfes retired from business, closing the mill at Pateley Bridge.

John B. Morrison and Arthur W. Metcalfe together managed the Ulster Spinning Co. with the Mackie family also on the Board and testing new machinery in the mill. They were followed by their respective sons Maynard Morrison, who became managing director, and Percy Metcalfe who was also on the Board. With business declining in the 1950s the Grove Mill closed and in the period 1956 to 1960 the Linfield Mill was also closed down.

John Barbour Morrison
Eileen Black

STEWARTS OF BALLYDRAIN

Captain William Stewart

John Stewart = Anna Wilson
1621–1691   1619–1682
BALLYDRAIN

Jane = George Stewart   Thomas Stewart = Martha
1668–1734   1666–1740   1660–1715   d. 1755
                               BALLYDRAIN

John Stewart = Jane Legge of Malone House
1701–1784   1698–1778
BALLYDRAIN

Elinor   Thomas Stewart = Mrs Harris   Martha Stewart = Israel Younghusband
1726–1806   1726–1806   1731–1758
                    of **WHITEHOUSE**

William Younghusband   John Younghusband = Letitia Black
                              1754–1843   1755–1833
                              owner of **BALLYDRAIN**
                              which he sold to Hugh Montgomery

Mary Isabella = Rev. John Clarke   Geo Alexander Stewart = Matilda Rainey   Jane Stewart = Walter Wilson
Stewart   1778–1805   of Greenock   1774–1849   of Croghlin
                                      NEWGROVE

Robert Henry Sturrock Reade DL = Dorothea Emily   Emelina Annabella Reade
1837–1913   1839–1921
WILMONT

James Stewart Reade = Emily Constance Jane Charley   Robert Sturrock Reade   Harold Ernest Reade = Mina St Clair Gray
1871–1934   1872–1955   1872–1872   1874–1926
CLONMORE

AND WILMONT

died 1641

daughter of Laird of Croghlin

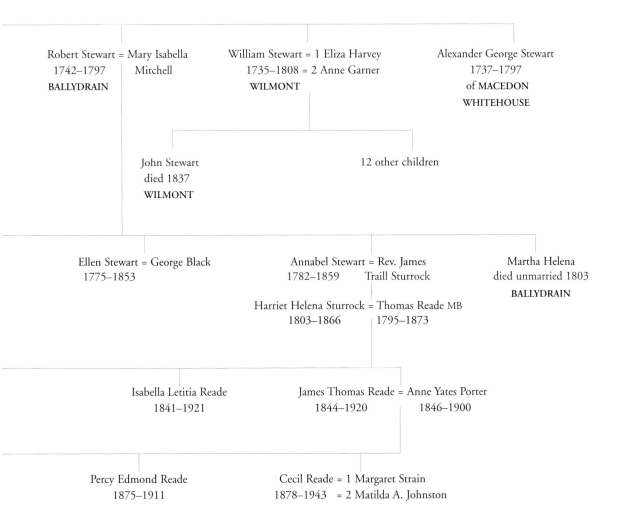

John Stewart = Eliza
will 1714

Florence Stewart = Thomas Martin
1655–1683   1643–1685

Robert Stewart = Mary Isabella
1742–1797   Mitchell
BALLYDRAIN

William Stewart = 1 Eliza Harvey
1735–1808 = 2 Anne Garner
WILMONT

Alexander George Stewart
1737–1797
of **MACEDON**
WHITEHOUSE

John Stewart
died 1837
WILMONT

12 other children

Ellen Stewart = George Black
1775–1853

Annabel Stewart = Rev. James
1782–1859   Traill Sturrock

Martha Helena
died unmarried 1803
BALLYDRAIN

Harriet Helena Sturrock = Thomas Reade MB
1803–1866   1795–1873

Isabella Letitia Reade
1841–1921

James Thomas Reade = Anne Yates Porter
1844–1920   1846–1900

Percy Edmond Reade
1875–1911

Cecil Reade = 1 Margaret Strain
1878–1943 = 2 Matilda A. Johnston

BELVEDERE

BELVEDERE is a late eighteenth-century house surrounded by mature woodland and situated on the Ballylesson Road close to Ballyaughlis cross roads, between Belfast and Lisburn. James Watson Hull purchased Belvedere in 1786 after his return from Bombay, where he had amassed a large fortune working with the East India Company. He rose rapidly in public life becoming successively Justice of the Peace for Counties Antrim, Down and Meath and High Sheriff of County Down. In 1793 James Watson Hull left for England selling Belvedere to Andrew Durham JP who must have been involved in the linen industry since in 1812 a Linen Board Meeting signed by bleachers included Andrew Durham of Belvedere. Andrew Durham was succeeded in Belvedere by his son Andrew Durham Jr, who in 1844 sold the house to Robert Callwell and records show that his widow Elizabeth still occupied the house in 1861.

Belvedere is a two-storey double-fronted classical Georgian building of four bays with a central porch of Tuscan columns; the walls are stucco painted white, quoins painted black, the roof hipped with four evenly spaced chimneys. There is a two-storey extension to the left of the house and a yard with stables at the back. The windows are Georgian glazed, 3-over-6 pane sashes upstairs, 6-over-6 pane sashes below.

Johnny Morrison, who owned Ballydrain, bought Belvedere in 1948 for his sister Doreen, wife of Brigadier Broadhurst. The lands comprising forty or fifty acres were on the other side of the River Lagan from Ballydrain. Belvedere was occupied by the Broadhurst family until 1993 when it was sold to Gordon Mackie, a director of the world famous company, James Mackie & Sons Ltd, which manufactured textile spinning and weaving machinery. He had also previously been a director of the Ulster Spinning Company.

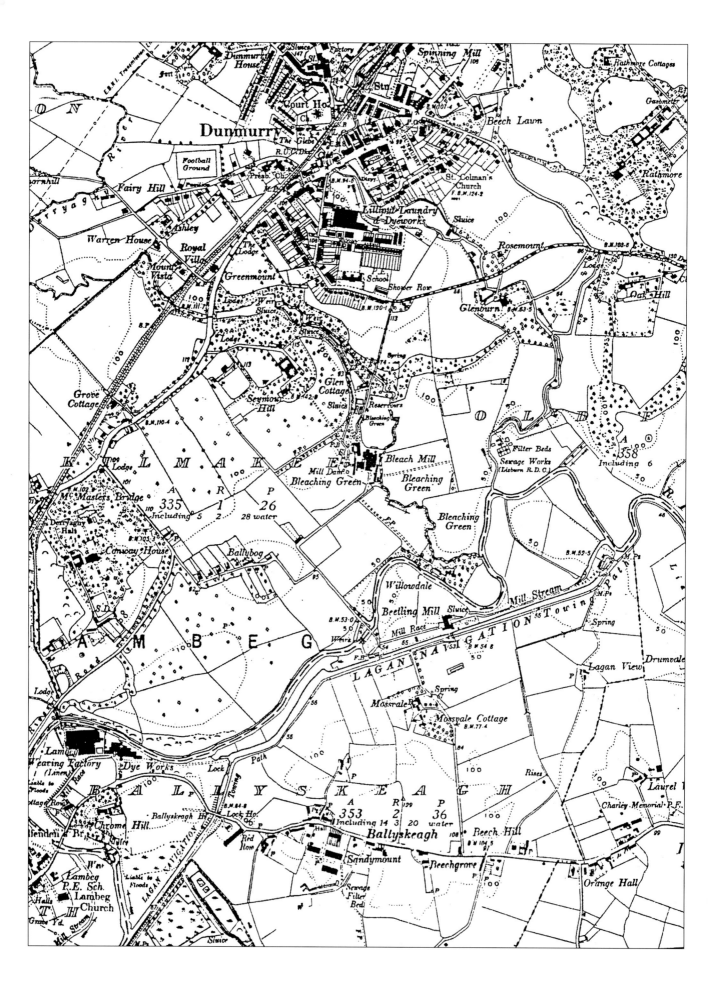

6

DUNMURRY

Seymour Hill
Drawn by Joseph Molloy, engraved by E.K. Proctor, 1832
Reproduced with the kind permission of the Linen Hall Library

Engraving of the Seymour
Hill bleachworks of J. & W.
Charley and Co. *c* 1850

PRONI

THE CHARLEYS
OF SEYMOUR HILL

FOR OVER 200 YEARS, members of the Charley family have lived in the
Dunmurry area, inter-marrying with neighbouring families connected with
the linen trade, such as the Wolfendens of Lambeg, the McCances, Richardsons,
Hunters, Herdmans, Riddells, Reades and Duffins. The Charleys were a
Lancashire family originally known as Chorley, some of whom fled to the North
of Ireland after taking part in the 1715 Jacobite Rebellion. The founder of the
Irish branch of the family appears to have been Ralph Charley (1674–1746), a
prosperous merchant in Belfast who in 1725 purchased Finaghy House, setting
up looms there to weave linen. The family owned several bleach greens in the
area and are credited with introducing the use of chlorine into the bleaching
process.

In 1783, John Charley of Finaghy House, having served his time in the linen
trade under Richard Wolfenden of Harmony Hill, Lambeg, married the boss's
daughter, Anne Jane, and later inherited the Wolfenden linen business. They had
three sons, John (1784–1844), Matthew (1788–1846) and William
(1790–1838), the business being continued by John and William who formed a
partnership in 1824 and traded as J. & W. Charley & Co. The eldest son John
died unmarried in 1844. John Charley's second son Matthew of Finaghy House,

Dunmurry, did not continue in the business; he was the father of the distinguished Sir William Charley, QC, MP (1833–1904) Common Sergeant of London.

In 1820 William Charley purchased and remodelled the bleach green at Dunmurry and also the nearby Mossvale works. Eventually the business was transferred to a new factory, which they built at Seymour Hill the house and bleach works which William had bought in 1822 from Robert Allen Johnston, the original owner who had built Seymour Hill in 1789. In 1822 the house at Seymour Hill was in a ruinous state but by 1825 William Charley had employed Mr John McHenry, architect, to remodel and reconstruct it at a cost of almost £5,000. Seymour Hill was named after the Marquess of Hertford's surname, as he then owned the ground rent of the four hundred acres surrounding the two-storey mansion and the parkland, which included a glen, through which ran the Derriaghy river.

William Charley was a founding member of the Northern Banking Company and chairman of J. & W. Charley & Co., linen merchants. In 1817 he married Isabella, the eldest daughter of William Hunter, JP, of Dunmurry and they had three sons and five daughters. William Charley died in 1838, when the business passed to his second son William Junior (1826–1890) the father of the last two directors of J. & W. Charley, Captain A.F. Charley of Seymour Hill and Colonel Harold R. Charley of Warren House, Dunmurry. In 1944 Captain Arthur Charley was felling trees in the parkland of Seymour Hill when he met with a tragic mishap causing his death. The bleach greens were taken over by Blackstaff and eventually J. & W. Charley & Co. merged with Barbour's Linen Thread since Colonel W.R.H. Charley, the only son of Colonel Harold Charley, wished to pursue an army career.

The Charley linen business was always a speciality one, confining itself to the finest and most luxurious qualities in all sorts of household linen goods and often carrying out commissions for the Royal Family.

John Charley of Finaghy House, 1784–1844.
Founder of the linen firm J. & W. Charley & Co. with his brother William, he was also Chairman of the Shareholders Committee of the Northern Banking Company.
Private Collection

CHARLEY

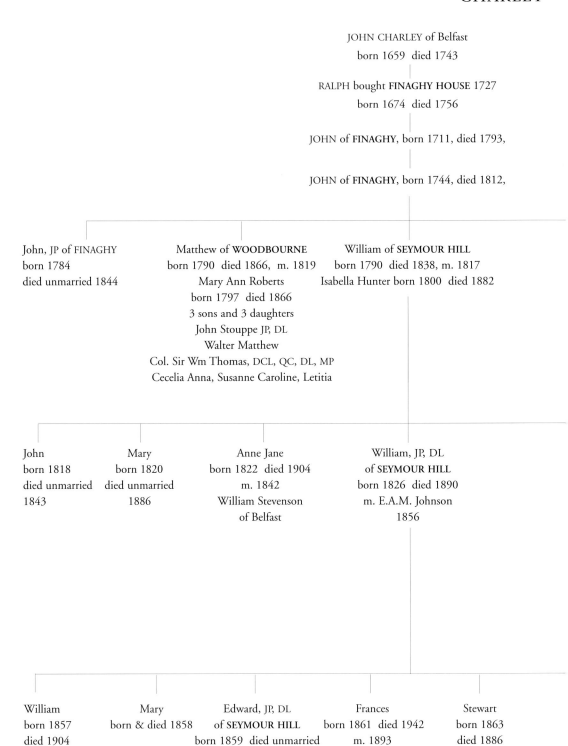

JOHN CHARLEY of Belfast
born 1659 died 1743

RALPH bought **FINAGHY HOUSE** 1727
born 1674 died 1756

JOHN of **FINAGHY**, born 1711, died 1793,

JOHN of **FINAGHY**, born 1744, died 1812,

John, JP of FINAGHY
born 1784
died unmarried 1844

Matthew of **WOODBOURNE**
born 1790 died 1866, m. 1819
Mary Ann Roberts
born 1797 died 1866
3 sons and 3 daughters
John Stouppe JP, DL
Walter Matthew
Col. Sir Wm Thomas, DCL, QC, DL, MP
Cecelia Anna, Susanne Caroline, Letitia

William of **SEYMOUR HILL**
born 1790 died 1838, m. 1817
Isabella Hunter born 1800 died 1882

John
born 1818
died unmarried
1843

Mary
born 1820
died unmarried
1886

Anne Jane
born 1822 died 1904
m. 1842
William Stevenson
of Belfast

William, JP, DL
of **SEYMOUR HILL**
born 1826 died 1890
m. E.A.M. Johnson
1856

William
born 1857
died 1904
in Australia
unmarried

Mary
born & died 1858

Edward, JP, DL
of **SEYMOUR HILL**
born 1859 died unmarried
1932

Frances
born 1861 died 1942
m. 1893
C.H. Duffin

Stewart
born 1863
died 1886

FAMILY TREE

m. twice and had 24 children

m. Elizabeth Hill, born 1683 died 1748

m. Jane Usher born 1718, died 1781
(+ 2 sons unmarried, 2 daughters married)

m. 1783 Anne Jane Wolfenden born 1758, died 1818

Edward	Annabella	Eliza Jane	Hill
born 1794	born 1793 died 1865	born 1800	born 1802 died 1848
died unmarried 1841	m. 1820 John Riddell	died unmarried	m. 1823 Mary Hunter, 6 sons & 2 daughters
	6 sons and 4 daughters	1864	John, Frederick, Wm Hunter,
			Henry Moore,
			Herdman, Hill, Edward, Mary, Edith

Edward	Elizabeth	Isabella	Emily
of **CONWAY**	born 1830 died 1913	born 1832 died 1905	born 1837
born 1827 died 1868	m. Andrew Caldecott	m. 1857	died unmarried
m. 1 Mary Caldecott 1852	4 sons & 6 daughters	Rev. R.L. Scott	
died 1854 1 daughter			
m. 2 Catherine Jane Richardson,			
born 1829 died 1906			
The Rev. Edward			
Ernest William Ralph			
Edith Margaret			
Kathleen Isobel Airth			

Thomas	Lizzie	Arthur, JP	Emily	Harold, CBE, DL	Maud
born 1866	born 1868	of **SEYMOUR HILL**	born 1872 died 1955	of **WARREN HOUSE**	born 1877
died 1885	died 1946	born 1870 died 1944	m. 1903	born 1875 died 1956	died 1918
	unmarried	m. Clare Fenn	J.S. Reade	m. 1923 Phyllis Hunter, MBE	m. 1905
			died 1934	born 1893 died 1988	

FINAGHY HOUSE

BALLYFINAGHY HOUSE, the seat of John Charley Esquire, is described by
Fagan in the *Ordnance Survey Memoirs* of 1837 as situated east of the turn-
pike road leading from Lisburn to Belfast, and in the Parish of Drumbeg. This
is the first recorded house of the Charley family having been purchased from a
Richard Woods in 1727 by Ralph Charley (1674–1756), a successful merchant
of Belfast. At that time Finaghy House was described as an imposing mansion
in a large park with extensive outhouses and stables, commanding a good view
of the surrounding scenery and in a demesne of about 75 English acres. The garden, about one English acre, was partly enclosed by a brick wall and partly by a

Drumbeg Church built 1798.
The spire was blown down 1831
The present spire was built
at the expense of the late,
JOHN CHARLEY, *of Finaghy,* 1833.
The Church was rebuilt 1870,–
the tower & spire being preserved.

THIS TABLET IS ERECTED IN MEMORY OF
HER UNCLE SAID JOHN CHARLEY.
BY A. J. STEVENSON.

Memorial to John Charley of
Finaghy in Drumbeg Parish Church

JFR

quickset fence, and contained a greenhouse and also glass frames for melons etc.

Five generations of the Charley family lived at Finaghy House until shortly after John Stouppe Charley (1825–1878) died when, in 1885, his widow Mrs Mary Stewart Charley (née Foster) sold the house and its contents. Latterly the house was described as two-storied with an outside castellated entrance porch and having six reception rooms and twelve bedrooms with appropriate ancillaries. A remarkable feature of two of the reception rooms was a revolving fireplace between the drawing room and the dining room. The Charley family armorial bearings were built into the outside gables and on a landing, half way up the wide oak bannistered stairs, the Coat of Arms is still engraved on the landing window.

Finaghy House is now known as Faith House, a comfortable home for senior citizens in the middle of a large housing estate off Finaghy Road South, Belfast.

Finaghy House, 2000
JFR

Charley family armorial bearings
built into outside gables
JFR

SEYMOUR HILL
DUNMURRY

SEYMOUR HILL stands on a hill facing south east across the Lagan Valley and to the south of the old main road from Belfast to Lisburn, easily visible from the M1 motorway. W.R.H. Charley, whose family occupied the house for 124 years until 1946, describes Seymour Hill as a large square Georgian house with four floors. The basement below ground level had extensive kitchens, scullery, larder, pantries, dairy rooms, wine cellars and a large servants' hall. On the ground floor the entrance hall had suits of armour standing in front of painted mural walls and there was a grandfather clock with the name William Charley in place of numerals. To the left of the front door was the dining room which contained the large family portraits, and behind the dining room was the cloak-room, gun room and butler's pantry. To the right of the front door was the drawing room and, behind it, a comfortable morning room and library. On the first floor were the main bedrooms, dressing rooms and bathroom. On the top floor were the day and night nurseries for the younger members of the family and also the staff sleeping quarters.

Brett describes the house as roughcast, painted grey and cream: five bays wide,

with heavy vermiculated double quoins, stone architraves and wide eaves brackets. He also mentions that two giant chimney stacks topping the hipped roof have seven large chimney-pots each, rather than the nine pots shown in old photographs. Dixon states that the entrance is within an acanthus-columned broken-pedimented porch embracing a semi-circular fanlight, now inscribed 'Seymour Hill House. 1990. BIH.', and this is at the head of six stone steps.

Doorway, early 1900s
ECA

A picture of life at Seymour Hill in the 1930s is given by W.R.H. Charley, who, as a child, frequently visited the house. 'In a small field behind the house there lived a pony called Ginger. Ginger, clad in large soft shoes, used to draw the grass cutting mower across the extensive lawns and tennis courts. In the summer, tennis parties were held on the four grass courts and the one hard court.' There was a large walled garden and grounds which were maintained by a head gardener and five or six under gardeners. This walled garden has now been renovated and is managed as the Seymour Hill Garden Project. Outside the walled garden was the Yew Tree Walk which led from the house down to the front drive entrance and between the house and walled garden were lawns and landscaped trees and shrubs. There were front and back avenues, the front drive entering via gates with a gate lodge, and in spring this avenue had daffodils all along the border from the gate to the main house. The Derriaghy river flowed

William Charley, 1790–1838
Private Collection

147

Seymour Hill bleach green of
J. & W. Charley & Co. *c* 1850

PRONI

William Charley JP, DL,
1826–1890

Private Collection

under the Belfast to Lisburn road into a lake within the grounds of Seymour Hill and was then divided into two mill races to work the factory water wheels. The main Derriaghy river continued down through the glen until it reached the River Lagan a short distance away near Mossvale where there was a bleach works.

Shortly after World War II the Northern Ireland Housing Trust was formed and, by the first vesting order issued in Northern Ireland, the Charley family was compelled to sell Seymour Hill House and all the grounds on the County Antrim side of the river Lagan. This was the first enterprise undertaken by the Trust, now the Northern Ireland Housing Executive, and in no time the house was surrounded by a well laid out but vast housing estate.

Seymour Hill House was converted into six flats. In 1986 the house was vandalised and badly damaged by firebombs and it was feared it might have to be pulled down. However, the Housing Executive transferred the listed building and part of the grounds to Belfast Improved Housing Association Ltd which successfully restored it to provide six one-person flats. The house was reopened by Colonel W.R.H. Charley, OBE, JP, DL on 12 October 1990.

Seymour Hill, 2000
JFR

CONWAY
DUNMURRY

THIS PROPERTY has already been mentioned in the ownership of the Barbour family who greatly altered Conway but it was built originally by a member of the Charley family.

Conway is situated on the south side of the old main Belfast to Lisburn road south of Dunmurry at Derriaghy. In 1852 William Charley of Seymour Hill gave some land from the Seymour Hill estate to his younger brother Edward (1827–1868), to build a house for his first wife Mary (née Caldecott) (1834–1854) from Essex. Edward named the house Conway after the local landowner the Marquess of Hertford, one of whose titles was Lord Conway.

The house is shown in this early photograph as it was originally built and before very considerable improvements were carried out by the Barbour family in the early years of the twentieth century.

Edward Charley's first wife Mary died in 1854 leaving one daughter and two years later he married Jane (née Richardson) (1829–1906) from Lambeg. After Edward's death in 1868 she continued to live in Conway with her four children and one stepdaughter until 1877. The house was leased by the Charleys to

William Reeves, Bishop of Down, Connor and Dromore, during his episcopate (1886–1892) until his death. In 1892 Conway was sold to John D. Barbour of Hilden, the father of Sir Milne Barbour, later Deputy Prime Minister of Northern Ireland.

MOSSVALE

Mossvale, *c* 1930s
Private Collection

MOSSVALE HOUSE was a nice old two-storey slated house down by the Lagan Canal which originally belonged to the owners of the local mill. The Charley family took over its ownership in 1820 when the mill and bleach works were purchased by William Charley (1790–1838) from Robert Johnston. The valuation books record a wash mill, boiling house, furnace house, bleaching house and drying house situated at the site. Mossvale House was on the County Down side of the Lagan, being encircled by trees and having stabling for ten horses.

For many years Mossvale House was the mill manager's house for the Charley bleach green. Latterly, after its closure, Captain Arthur Charley (1870–1944) lived there with his wife for several years after World War I before moving into The Lodge, Dunmurry. In 1936 the property was rented to a flamboyant gentleman who had some horses and put them in the stables. After heavily insuring the house and his horses this gentleman soaked piles of rags with paraffin around the house and stables. He then set fire to them and succeeded in burning the house to the ground. Fortunately passers-by saw the fire and managed to rescue the frightened horses.

The land and ruins of Mossvale remained in the Charley family for another fifty years until it was sold in the 1980s and a new house has been built on the site.

Engraving of bleach green at
Mossvale, *c* 1850

PRONI

WILLOWDALE

WILLOWDALE is approached by a sweeping tree lined driveway, bordering the River Lagan, off the Ballybog Road, Dunmurry and in the Lagan Valley Regional Park. The house, set in grounds of twenty acres, lies in a wooded triangle formed by the river Lagan and near the point where the Derriaghy river flows into the river Lagan, with mature trees shielding it from view both from the Seymour Hill housing estate and the M1 motorway.

Willowdale is a two-storey, five-bay Georgian farmhouse thought to be late eighteenth century and with a slated roof between chimney stacks at the gable ends. The entrance is flanked by rusticated pilasters rising to entablature, elaborate looped fanlight and triple keystone, surrounding a mahogany front door. The thick stone walls are covered in whitened roughcast with the quoins, window surrounds and door surround painted black. There is a two-storey return at the rear. At the front of the house there is a wide sweep of gravel allowing room for cars to turn and, beyond, flowering shrubs and mature trees on the bank of the Lagan.

W.R.H. Charley records that on entering the house there is a wide hall with a passage to the rear and the drawing room and dining room to left and right. The drawing room had an Adam type fireplace with a large grate suitable for burning large sized logs. Behind the two large front rooms are a breakfast room, a mistress's pantry, cloakroom and a large kitchen with scullery and pantry off it. The wide staircase leads to a large landing with four bedrooms, a dressing room and a bathroom.

Fagan, in the *Ordnance Survey Memoirs* of 1837, records Laganvale, the seat of William Lewson Esquire, as being situated on the banks of the Lagan and about two and a half miles from Lisburn. The garden, about two English acres, is enclosed by a quickset fence partly, and by the Lagan and Derriaghy rivers. Since Willowdale has a setting at exactly this point it would appear that it was previously called Laganvale. Fagan also mentions that the place was formerly the site of an extensive bleach green, which had to be relinquished many years ago in consequence of its supply of water being drawn off to swell the navigation.

Willowdale has been part of the Charley Estate since the early 1820s and has been occupied by tenants: Bassett records a Captain W. Kirk in residence in 1888. From 1939 to 1952 it was lived in by Mr & Mrs George Graham, and the house was sold in 1952 to Mr & Mrs Taylor, and Mrs Taylor remained there until 1999.

PHOENIX LODGE

PHOENIX LODGE was situated on the eastern side of the main Belfast to Lisburn road just south of Dunmurry. The house was Georgian style, rough-cast, painted white, of two storeys and three bays with a two-storey porch at the front. Label moulding was present at the top of the sashed and silled windows which retained their glazing bars. The roof was gabled with shallow eaves and moulded cornice.

In 1837 the Ulster Railway Company opened its first railway line from Belfast to Lisburn and to encourage the use of the railway, free passes were offered to people if they built new homes near the stations and halts. It is thought that this may have influenced William Charley (1790–1838) to build Phoenix Lodge for his daughter, Anne Jane, in 1837 shortly before he died. In 1842 Anne Jane Charley married William Stevenson of Belfast and they lived at Phoenix Lodge until his death in 1855. Mrs Stevenson then moved to live with her widowed mother, Mrs Isabella Charley, at Huntley, Upper Dunmurry Lane.

The name of the house was changed to The Lodge after the Phoenix Park murders in Dublin when Lord Frederick Cavendish and Thomas Burke, Chief Secretary & Under Secretary of Ireland, were assassinated. Captain Arthur Charley, JP (1870–1944), lived in The Lodge with his wife Clare after World War I until his brother Edward Charley, JP, DL (1859–1932) died and he moved into Seymour Hill. In the 1930s and at the beginning of World War II, The Lodge was rented by Lord and Lady Ampthill and in 1940 Major General Sir

James and Lady Cooke-Collis lived there. He was the first Ulster Agent in London but died in 1941 as a result of a German air raid on his club in London. Major General Majendie, the GOC Northern Ireland District, next occupied The Lodge.

Finally in 1947 the house was bought by Mrs Helen Reilly Harland, a sister of Sir Milne Barbour of Conway, and a daughter of John Doherty Barbour. She had firstly married Thomas Andrews, managing director and chief designer at Harland and Wolff's. Mr Andrews was lost when the *Titanic*, which he had designed, went down in the North Atlantic in April, 1912. Later she married Henry Harland of Aldenham, Herts. Mrs Harland took up residence at The Lodge to be near her brother, the late Sir Milne Barbour and she died there on 22nd August 1966.

After her mother's death Elba Andrews lived at The Lodge until the late 1960s. The house was put on the market but was vested, in spite of the fact that it was a listed building, and the grounds taken over for the expansion of a nearby factory, leaving the large weeping ash tree that dominated the front lawn as all that remains of The Lodge.

Wedding of Thomas Andrews, son of the Rt Hon. J. Andrews of Comber (linen) and Miss Helen Barbour, daughter of John D. Barbour of Conway, Dunmurry which took place on 24 June 1908 at Lambeg Parish Church. Thomas Andrews was managing director of Harland and Wolff and designer of the *Titanic*. He lost his life in the *Titanic* disaster, 1912, leaving a widow and baby daughter, Elizabeth.

NMGNI UM

WOODBOURNE HOUSE

WOODBOURNE was a house near Suffolk, in the Parish of Upper Falls, which came into the Charley family when it was given to Mary Ann Roberts (1797–1866) on her marriage in 1819 to Matthew Charley (1788–1846) by her father Walter Roberts of Collin House. He had rebuilt the house on the site of an old farmhouse at the spot known as Crooke's Ford. Woodbourne was so named because of the wood, or glen, on one side and a burn, the Lady's River, on the other. In the twentieth century the house was a commodious two-storey slated building with an older section on the right hand side set back but continuous with the main building and a large conservatory on the left hand side of the building. Surrounding the house was a lawn filled with shrubs and trees with an adjoining walled garden and orchard.

Woodbourne had a large sunlit entrance hall with folding doors two thirds of the way back from the front door to screen off the stairs and back passages and on the folding screen was the Charley Coat of Arms. The stairs led in a spiral curve to a lobby the same size as the hall lit by a large window. On the first floor bedrooms led off the lobby and on the top floor was a long low playroom, running over a third of the house.

Matthew and Mary Charley brought up their six children at Woodbourne before taking over the senior family house Finaghy House on the death of Matthew's elder brother John (1784–1844). In 1844 Woodbourne was taken over by their son John Stouppe Charley (1825–1878) who married in 1851 Mary Stewart Foster (1832–1915) a daughter of Francis Foster JP of Roshin Lodge, Co. Donegal. John Stouppe Charley took over Finaghy House on his mother's death in 1866. John and Matthew Charley were both original shareholders of the Northern Bank, John being Chairman of the Bank Committee from 1842 to 1844. John Stouppe Charley succeeded his uncle John on the committee of the Northern Banking Co. in 1845 and he was also a JP and DL for counties Antrim and Donegal and High Sheriff of Co. Donegal in 1875.

From 1878, on John Stouppe Charley's death, various family connections lived in Woodbourne until the late 1890s when it was occupied by John Stouppe Finlay McCance (1865–1926) until his death. Finlay McCance married Mary Letitia Bristow and they had three sons and one daughter born at Woodbourne. Subsequently Woodbourne was lived in by various members of the Charley and McCance families. Soon after World War II it became a popular hotel but in the mid-1970s, after suffering bomb damage, it was converted into a fortified RUC station.

The Parish of Upper Falls was constituted in 1859 and the Church of St John the Baptist was built on land belonging to and adjacent to Woodbourne, given by John Stouppe Charley.

WARREN HOUSE

Warren House
Private Collection

WARREN HOUSE is situated south of Dunmurry on the northern side of the Belfast to Lisburn road. The house was originally known as Warren View and was a small house on the Charley estate which, until 1922, was occupied by different members of the Johnston family; Bassett records a Samuel Johnston in residence in 1888. Warren House looked across the Derriaghy River to an ancient mound and rabbit warren, and it had a good garden.

In 1923 Edward Charley of Seymour Hill gave Warren House to his brother

Colonel Harold Charley, CBE, DL (1875–1956) on his marriage to Phyllis Hunter MBE (1893–1988). They added to the house and enlarged it over several years, resulting in a variety of window styles in this two-storey, slated Victorian house. In 1951 the house was sold by the Charleys and bought by the winner of a large football pool prize, who again sold it. In 1970, when the De Lorean factory was built in nearby fields, Warren House was fitted out for John De Lorean to live in; however it is now occupied by new owners.

Mrs Phyllis Charley, age 3
Private Collection

HUNTLEY

HUNTLEY is situated on Upper Dunmurry Lane and was originally known as Huntley Lodge. The house is two-storey, mid-nineteenth century, with a slated roof, walls are smooth rendered and windows have Georgian glazed sashes. An imposing entrance has eared architraves and keystone contained in a square projecting pilastered porch.

Huntley was built about 1830 by William Hunter (1777–1856) of Dunmurry House on land leased by the Stewarts of Ballydrain from the Donegall estates. William (1806-1890), his son, lived in Huntley for a time and brought up his family there until, in the mid 1850s, he moved to the Isle of Man.

The house was then left by his father William Hunter to his widowed sister, Mrs Isabella Charley (1800–1882). Isabella's husband, William Charley of Seymour Hill, had died in 1838, and she had lived in Seymour Hill until her eldest son William was married in 1856. Isabella moved to Huntley where she was joined by three of her daughters, Mary (1820–1886), Anne Jane Stevenson (1822–1904), whose husband had died in 1855, and Emily (1837–1917). W.R.H. Charley states that for many years, every Sunday, the Charleys of

Seymour Hill would travel in the family coach to visit their grandmother and aunts for afternoon tea at Huntley.

The ladies at Huntley were talented artists, did embroidery, and kept beautiful scrap books. Many charities were supported by the ladies and they gave generously to local churches, schools and church halls. In 1892 they founded the Charley Memorial School at Drumbeg in memory of their brother William Charley (1826–1890) of Seymour Hill and also the Stevenson Memorial School in Dunmurry.

Miss Emily Charley died in 1917 and Huntley was let on a 20 year lease to James Cowie, who, in 1927, answered an advertisement by an estate agent for a house in the country but within easy reach of Belfast. This resulted in G. Herbert Bryson taking on the remainder of the lease which had 10 years still to run. In February 1928 Herbert Bryson married Rosemary Buckby Sinton, daughter of Frederick B. Sinton, linen bleacher, of Banford House, Gilford, Co. Down. Herbert Bryson's description of the house at the time of his marriage is of interest:

> Huntley is a Regency house, the main rooms well proportioned and with fine plaster mouldings, but the back premises had never been touched since the house was built. In the kitchen there was a range which burned a ton of coal every two weeks in winter or in three weeks in summer; but as coal cost under two pounds a ton, this was not important.

Huntley remained in the possession of the Charley family until 1932, when Edward Charley JP, DL (1859–1932) of Seymour Hill died, and the property was sold to G. Herbert Bryson, a director of Spence Bryson & Co., Ltd. In the twenty-first century Huntley continues in Bryson family ownership.

Mrs Isabella Charley
Private Collection

Charley Memorial Primary School, Drumbeg, founded 1892

JFR

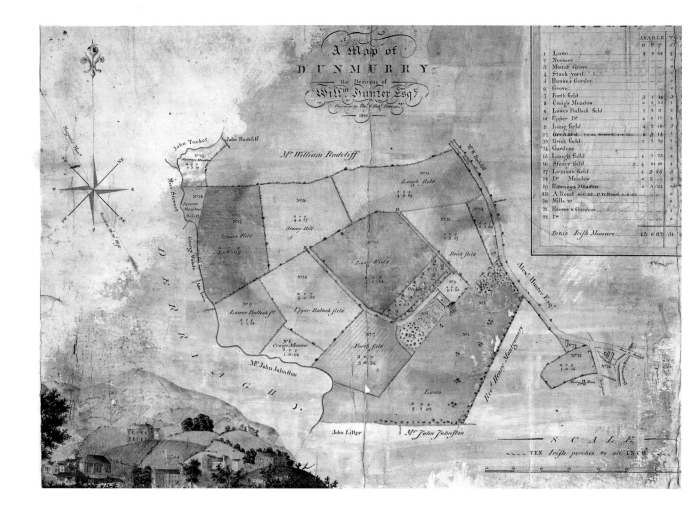

THE HUNTERS OF DUNMURRY

A map of Dunmurry, the demesne of William Hunter, Esq., 1816, with a painting of Dunmurry House, overlooking the linen factory.

PRONI

THERE IS EVIDENCE to suggest that the first Hunter resident in the Lagan Valley was Alexander Hunter of Straidarran, Scotland, a military gentleman who was rewarded for his services to Cromwell or the crown by a gift of land at Dunmurry, Co. Antrim. Lisburn Cathedral records show the baptism on 12 July 1663 of John, son of Alexander Hunter, Derriaghy. However, on the pattern of Scotch settlers in Ireland in the seventeenth century, Alexander, being a good Presbyterian brought all sorts of friends and neighbours from his old home, and kept them about him. This brought the odd result of a strong Presbyterian community at Dunmurry, in the middle of what was the Chichester or English settlement of the Lagan Valley. In consequence the First Presbyterian (now Non-Subscribing) Church, Dunmurry was established about 1678.

John Hunter became a bleacher at Glenmore, Lambeg, residing in Castle Street, Lisburn, and was for many years a Trustee of the estate of the Marquess of Hertford. For over one hundred years encompassing the period from the mid-eighteenth to the mid-nineteenth centuries the Hunter family owned bleach greens in and around Dunmurry. William Hunter (1712–1771) is recorded in the *Ordnance Survey Memoirs* as establishing the Dunmurry bleach green in the mid-eighteenth century with a house and demesne of thirty English acres at The Green. The house was rebuilt and enlarged by his son William (1745–1801) and in 1837 when occupied by Alexander Hunter it was described in the *Ordnance Survey Memoirs* as a commodious double house, two storeys high and slated, entrance from the village by two good iron gates. The grounds about the house were sheltered and ornamented by a variety of forest trees, laurels and evergreens with the garden containing a greenhouse sixty feet long.

The ground occupied by the bleach green, which was established at Dunmurry in the middle of the eighteenth century by William Hunter (1712–1772) and continued by his son, William (1745–1801), was recorded as twenty-six English acres, with an average of 11,000 linen webs annually bleached giving employment to fifty labourers. William Hunter (1745–1801), also owned a corn mill and a flax mill at Dunmurry but the flax mill became disused and the size of the corn mill was doubled. William Hunter(1745–1801) married Mary Riddell and had at least four children who were destined to become involved in the linen trade. His eldest son, William (1777–1856), developed the corn mills and set up a flour mill in Dunmurry which used a steam engine to grind flour in the event of there not being sufficient water power. William appears to have been very successful in business and built Dunmurry House in 1815 in a demesne of ninety-six English acres. He acquired Glenburn bleach green for his son William Hunter Junior (1806–1890), who was running it in 1837, while living at Huntley Lodge, Upper Dunmurry Lane, a house which had been built by his father in 1830.

Detail from a map of Dunmurry with a painting of Dunmurry House, overlooking the linen factory.

PRONI

In 1837 the business was carried on by Alexander Hunter (1787–1878),

youngest son of William Hunter, who continued to live in his father's house at 'The Green' with his wife Betsy, daughter of James Steen of Clady. Alexander Hunter (1787–1878), continued his father and grandfather's business of bleaching linen, employing fifty men to work a water driven washmill with two beetling engines. Alexander's eldest son, William Steen Hunter (1812–1863) was educated at the Royal Belfast Academical Institution and was reputed to be a splendid horseman; he was nominally apprenticed in his father's extensive bleach green. When William came of age his father sent him on a tour to America with some gentlemen and during his absence his father purchased for him a bleach green on which was a comfortable house. This was Duneight House, overlooking a small lake, beside the Ravarnet river which flows into the river Lagan south of Lisburn. The river provided power for a beetling mill which Alexander Hunter had built in 1833 and by 1836 William Steen Hunter is recorded as a linen merchant and bleacher at Duneight.

In the period following 1850 and the Irish famine there was fierce competition in the linen industry of the Lagan Valley with the growth of the large companies such as York Street Flax Spinning Co., William Ewart & Son, J. & W. Charley, J.N. Richardson, Sons & Owden, and William Barbour & Sons. William Hunter of Dunmurry House died in 1856, leaving his lands and mills to his son James, and thereafter the Hunter businesses went into steep decline. William Steen Hunter set off for Canada to try to retrieve the family fortune, but he died there in 1863. However, in 1862 his wife Anna opened a boarding and day school in Castle Street, Lisburn, in order to support their large family. This school was very successful and in time led to the establishment of Princess Gardens School, University Street, Belfast and eventually after a considerable further period of years to Hunterhouse College, Dunmurry, established at Strathearne House, a former Barbour linen house.

The Hunter linen business appears to have ceased in 1871 with bankruptcy papers being filed for James Hunter and encumbered estate sale to Joseph Richardson, Wakefield Haughton Dixon, Robert Laurence Hamilton and James Theodore Richardson.

HUNTER FAMILY TREE

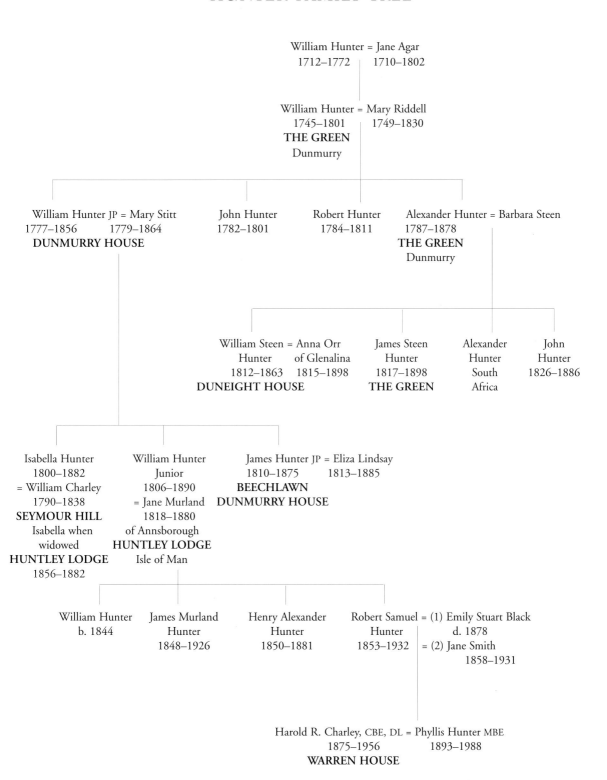

William Hunter = Jane Agar
1712–1772   1710–1802

William Hunter = Mary Riddell
1745–1801   1749–1830
THE GREEN
Dunmurry

William Hunter JP = Mary Stitt
1777–1856   1779–1864
DUNMURRY HOUSE

John Hunter
1782–1801

Robert Hunter
1784–1811

Alexander Hunter = Barbara Steen
1787–1878
THE GREEN
Dunmurry

William Steen = Anna Orr
Hunter   of Glenalina
1812–1863   1815–1898
DUNEIGHT HOUSE

James Steen
Hunter
1817–1898
THE GREEN

Alexander
Hunter
South
Africa

John
Hunter
1826–1886

Isabella Hunter
1800–1882
= William Charley
1790–1838
SEYMOUR HILL
Isabella when
widowed
HUNTLEY LODGE
1856–1882

William Hunter
Junior
1806–1890
= Jane Murland
1818–1880
of Annsborough
HUNTLEY LODGE
Isle of Man

James Hunter JP = Eliza Lindsay
1810–1875   1813–1885
BEECHLAWN
DUNMURRY HOUSE

William Hunter
b. 1844

James Murland
Hunter
1848–1926

Henry Alexander
Hunter
1850–1881

Robert Samuel = (1) Emily Stuart Black
Hunter   d. 1878
1853–1932   = (2) Jane Smith
                        1858–1931

Harold R. Charley, CBE, DL = Phyllis Hunter MBE
1875–1956   1893–1988
WARREN HOUSE

DUNMURRY HOUSE

WILLIAM HUNTER's eldest son, William (1777–1856), is recorded in the *Ordnance Survey Memoirs* as living at Dunmurry House which was situated west of the road leading from Lisburn to Belfast. The house was described as a commodious brick edifice, two storeys high and slated, of oblong shape with wings and rear buildings attached, the entrance to the house being by a handsome winding avenue from the Falls Road. The demesne contained about 96 English acres, laid out in well enclosed fields, with the house and gardens sheltered on the north, west and south by plantations. William Hunter built the house, at that time known as The Fort, in 1815 and subsequently continued to improve the garden and make plantings, developing the demesne. Dunmurry House was situated on a hill so that the house commanded a view of the surrounding countryside and it was situated between two raths.

William Hunter was the proprietor of the Dunmurry flour and corn mills in the village of Dunmurry. He also owned bleach greens in the neighbourhood and was a wealthy business man. Dunmurry House continued in the Hunter family ownership until 1885 when the property was sold to James D. Boyd, who later, about 1900, had two gate lodges built at the entrances to the house.

In the twentieth century Dunmurry House was again occupied by men who were involved in the manufacture of linen. Thomas D. Paul, managing director of the Grove Weaving Co., Ltd, acquired the property in the mid 1920s and lived there until his death in November 1935. Mrs T.D. Paul lived on at Dunmurry House until 1955 when she sold the property to Alexander Davison (1895–1984) who had succeeded her husband as managing director at the Grove

Weaving Co., Ltd, Beersbridge Road, Belfast.

At this time Dunmurry House was very commodious having five reception rooms, with kitchen and a corridor to a further four rooms. The first floor had six bedrooms and in the Davisons' time two of these were a 'nanny' suite while the second floor contained a further four bedrooms. During this period the property was staffed by a cook, two maids, a nanny, two gardeners and a chauffeur. The grounds contained a walled garden, along with long greenhouses and numerous potting sheds, providing a very considerable play area for the five Davison children.

In 1963 the Housing Executive requisitioned land from the estate for the building of houses and the Davisons left Dunmurry House which was subsequently converted into flats and was later demolished.

Alexander Davison
LL

DUNEIGHT HOUSE

Duneight House, Blaris
JFR

ALEXANDER HUNTER of Dunmurry bought a damask bleach green and built a beetling mill in 1833 at Duneight beside the Ravarnet River. His son William Steen Hunter (1812–1863) married Anna Orr (1815–1898) in 1836 and Alexander gave him Duneight House, setting him up as a linen merchant and bleacher. Duneight House was described as a comfortable house overlooking a small lake. The bleach green and house were situated south-east of Lisburn and adjacent to Ravarnet. However, by 1860 there was considerable competition in the linen industry of the Lagan Valley with the growth of the large companies such as Barbour's, Richardson's, Charley's and McCance's, and the Hunters sold Duneight in 1862.

Duneight House, to the front, is a three-bay, two-storey house, possibly dating from the 1830s when Alexander Steen Hunter took up residence. Brett states that to the rear, and at right angles to the front is the original, probably mid-eighteenth-century, house. He also describes the front as 'stuccoed, with quoins,

Duneight House, *c* 1880
Private Collection

complicated architraves round the windows with Greek key pattern mouldings, and Regency style glazing bars'.

GLENBURN

Glenburn
JFR

The present Glenburn is a late-Georgian house, part of the building predating the first Ordnance Survey map of 1832–33, and is situated off Upper Dunmurry Lane just south of Dunmurry in Old Forge townland. The house is two-storey, five-bay with a hipped and slated roof and walls painted white, the main elevation facing south-west and having a neat portico of four columns. The building is currently in institutional use but, when in residential use in 1861, it was described as containing four sitting rooms, nine bedrooms and bathroom together with servants' hall and apartments, an excellent kitchen with commodious range, pantries etc., all of modern erection. An auction brochure of 1861 describes Glenburn Mansion and Demesne, Dunmurry, as being suitable in every respect for a gentleman's country seat, having a demesne of seventy-five acres, and a tastefully laid out garden which was well stocked with fruit trees. On the south side of the house was a water dam which had been ornamented by the planting of shrubs and nearby a tea house surrounded by a garden.

DARBY & CURTEIS
LISBURN.

John Wolfenden, a bleacher, established Glenburn bleach green about 1745 and originally lived in Rosemount, a house on the Glenburn demesne. Subsequently, he built nearby the house named Glenburn and continued to bleach on the green. After John Wolfenden, Glenburn Mansion was occupied by John Hogg, followed by Mr Derby and next by Edward Curtis who enlarged the house considerably in 1818. He was a linen merchant and bleacher, who lived there for at least twenty years until the house became the residence of Major Crossley, JP, about 1838. By the early 1850s the house at Glenburn was occupied by James McConnell of McConnell & Kennedy, flax and tow spinners, Millvale, Falls Road. Yet another occupant by the mid-1860s was Isaac J. Murphy of John Murphy & Co., flax spinners, Linfield Mill.

Early in the nineteenth century William Hunter of Dunmurry took a lease of the Glenburn bleach green and in 1837 it was being run by William Hunter Junior of Dunmurry, with an average of 11,000 linen webs being bleached annually and employing twenty-eight men. The bleach grounds occupied 30 acres and comprised bleach mills, beetling works and bleach green with a good supply of water from the Glen river. In addition the Rahery Beetling Mill stood in the grounds of Rosemount on the Glenburn Estate and, in 1861, Alexander Hunter was named as tenant.

Glenburn was sold in 1889 to Major General Clarke so ending the connection to the linen industry. The house is presently used as the Belfast Bible College.

AUCTIONS.

Valuable Freehold Property for Sale
IN THE COUNTY ANTRIM,

Situate Four Miles from Belfast, on the Great Mail Coa Road to Dublin, and 2½ from Lisburn,

THE MANSION HOUSE and DEMESN LANDS of GLENBURNE, in the Upper H Barony of Belfast, containing 135 Acres, English Statu Measure, held for Lives renewable for ever, at the Year Rent of £56. The Lands are fully cropped and in hi order. On these Premises are Sixteen COTTAGE and a BLEACH-GREEN, at present in full occupatio capable of Bleaching 14,000 pieces of Linen yearly, with never failing supply of Spring Water; and every artic used in Bleaching can be brought by the Canal from Be fast and landed within a few perches of the works, whic are at present in such good order as not to require for mar years any repair. Attached to the Bleach-Green are Lin Offices, with an excellent Oak Screw Press, capable containing 140 pieces of Linen, with various other Press and conveniences.

The Demesne is highly ornamented by water and mar thousand Forest Trees, (all registered,) of 30 years' growt including valuable Oak and Ash; also some hundreds of ol Trees, fit for timber. There is likewise an excellent wal ed Garden and Shrubbery, with an Orchard and Nutte attached to it, containing nearly Three Acres, all in goo bearing—also an Ice House. Attached to the Farm Yar is a Threshing Mill of four-horse power, turned by wate The beauty and convenience of the above Grounds are to well known to need further comment; such a situatio either for a private Gentleman's residence, or for one cor nected extensively in the Linen Trade, is rarely to be me with. The Bleach-Green, with 30 Acres of Groun could, with very little inconvenience, be detached from th Demesne.

There is also attached to GLENBURNE a FARM, cor taining nearly 80 Acres, English Statute Measure, at pre sent fully cropped, and in excellent condition, with a com fortable small DWELLING-HOUSE and OFFICES Seven years of the Lease unexpired. This the purchase of Glenburne may have or not as he thinks proper.

To accommodate the purchaser, a part of the purchase money may remain secured on the Premises.

Application to be made to the Proprietor, E. CUR TEIS, Esq. GLENBURNE. (12

The above Property will be SOLD by AUC

Notice of auction of Mansion House and Demesne Lands of Glenburne

Belfast News Letter
13 June 1834

RATHMORE
DUNMURRY

Rathmore, 1999

JFR

RATHMORE HOUSE, situated on the main Belfast to Lisburn Road between Finaghy and Dunmurry, has been described by Paul Larmour as a substantial mid-Victorian house built of sandstone, Italianate in style with Tuscan columned porch and a very impressive copper-vaulted hall with coloured roof light and Corinthian colonnade. In family records, 'Etablissements Victor Coates, Paris', the architect of Rathmore is given as Paxton but Larmour describes the house as probably by Lanyon, Lynn and Lanyon, built for Victor Coates, JP, DL, in 1870. The author of the family record states: 'it was quite modern with light from the roof and central heating; the first in Ireland and considered for many years most unhealthy. The rooms were too large to be heated by fires and this central heating made the house too comfortable.' Rathmore House was built on a hill at Kingsway, Dunmurry in a park of one hundred and twenty acres previously occupied by Huntley Cottage. The front drive was a mile and a quarter long and the house had two gate lodges, along with extensive

stables, gas works, gardens and greenhouses. Mature and exotic trees remain in the grounds.

Victor Coates, son of William Coates, JP of Glentoran, married Margaret Airth Richardson, daughter of Jonathan Richardson, MP, of Lambeg House, Lambeg in 1863. Victor Coates's family were iron founders and in his time Coates & Company became the most important steam engine and boiler manufacturers in Ireland, supplying numerous local mills, factories and pumping stations and exporting engines. In fact Victor Coates was very forward looking, hence the installation of central heating in Rathmore. The Coates family lived in style with inside staff of three menservants and nine maids, while outside staff comprised a head gardener, his workmen, grooms and helpers, farm manager and labourers.

Victor Coates lived at Rathmore for forty years and following his death his widow continued to occupy the house as shown in the valuation records of 1912. Rathmore was subsequently purchased by Samuel McCrudden JP, who had linen interests. During World War II the house was used by Messrs Harland & Wolff, who had drawing offices erected in the grounds. Rathmore House is now a flourishing Grammar School, catering for 1,400 pupils.

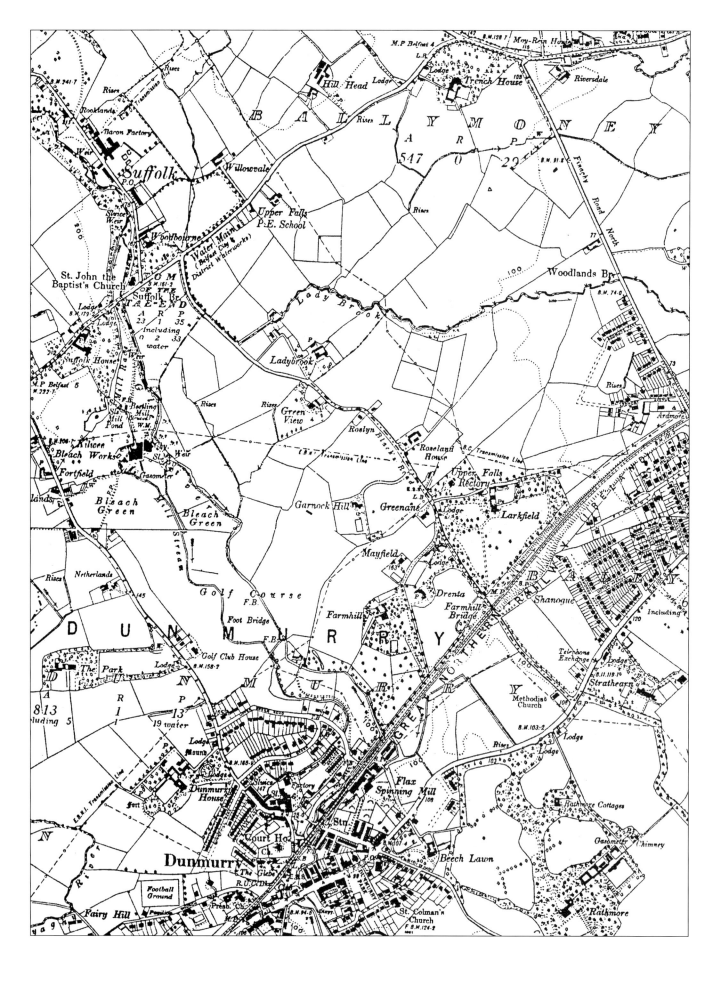

7

FINAGHY

Suffolk House
Drawn by Joseph Molloy, engraved by E.K. Proctor, 1832
Reproduced with the kind permission of the Linen Hall Library

THE McCANCES OF SUFFOLK

DAVID McCANCE (1684–1747) and his younger brother William (1693–1758) almost certainly came from Co. Down where there were McCances in Donaghadee, Comber, Greyabbey and Ballynahinch earlier than this in the 17th century. The family is reputed to have come originally from Scotland although the name is almost unknown in Scotland at the present time. David McCance had an estate called in early leases Mulliganstown, also known as Ballycullo, a place name which now seems to be extinct. It lay somewhere between the modern Belfast Lisburn Road and the Upper Falls Road, alongside Black's Road. The little Glen river, only some four miles long, flowed rapidly from Colin Hill to the Lagan, through Dunmurry, and in its short length, by the aid of storage dams, eventually supplied water for at least six bleach greens. David McCance had only one child, a son John (1711–1786) who was, almost certainly, in the linen trade as a linen draper, and later as a bleacher, and succeeded his father in Mulliganstown.

John McCance left four surviving children as follows:

1 David (b. 1738) ancestor of the Knocknagoney family, who apparently were not connected with the linen trade;

2 Mary (b. 1743) married the Rev. James Stouppe, a Presbyterian minister of Dunmurry but lived at Glenville and was in the linen trade. They had a son John McCance Stouppe (1778–1819) who ran the bleach green at Glenville, in the townland of Ballycullo. He married his first cousin Mary, only daughter of John McCance of Farmhill;

3 John of Farmhill, Dunmurry (1744–1811) married in 1771 Jane Charley of Seymour Hill and had one son John (1772–1835) and one daughter Mary. John McCance, their son, became a distinguished Member of Parliament for Belfast; unfortunately he lived for only four months after taking his seat;

4   William (1746–1810) worked extensively in the linen trade with works at
    Kilwee and a bleach green and residence at Suffolk.

John McCance Stouppe married the sister of John McCance MP and took
up residence at Glenville where bleaching was still carried out, as it had
been at Suffolk for some time by William, the uncle of John McCance
MP. John McCance Stouppe traded in partnership with his cousin and
brother-in-law as McCance and Stouppe, and on his death without children he left Glenville and his share in the business to his partner. The
name Stouppe is not an Irish one and James Stouppe may have been a
Huguenot linen merchant or the Rev James Stouppe may have come over
with William III's army and settled in the area. The Stouppes were a highly respected family in Dunmurry where James was the Presbyterian minister. The name has lingered on in John Stouppe Charley of Finaghy and
John Stouppe Finlay McCance (1865–1926).

   From an early age John McCance MP had interests in public affairs and
local government outside the family linen business. As a merchant banker
he became the chairman of the shareholder's committee from the time
when the Bank of Montgomery, Orr and Sloane, in which he was a partner, was incorporated in 1824 to form the Northern Banking Co., until
his death. As early as 1801 he was a Magistrate and became High Sheriff
of County Down in 1825 and of County Antrim in 1827; he was also a
Police Commissioner, Vice-President of the Belfast Academy, and a
Trustee of the Botanic Gardens. Suffolk House, at this time, was the centre of much social activity, with many balls being held in the house in the
spring and summer months. John McCance was a keen sportsman and very
interested in horses and hounds, keeping a pack of hounds and hunting the
Kilultagh country. The McCance Hunt Cup in the Ulster Museum is dated
1829 and inscribed: 'Presented by Wm. Coates, John Charley, George Suffern,
J. Johnson, Alexander Arthur, Isaac Hardy, Murray Suffern to John McCance
Esq., as a slight but sincere tribute to express their high sense of the kind atten-
tion which they have experienced while hunting with his hounds.'

Stained glass window in
Dunmurry Non-Subscribing
Presbyterian Church representing
Colin Glen. In memory of John
Wellington Stouppe McCance
and Henry Jones McCance.

JFR

   John McCance married three times, firstly to Maria Finlay of Carrickfergus,
when they lived at Roselands, but she died after the birth of their son William;
secondly to Jane Russell, youngest daughter of John Russell of Edenderry,
County Down, who died childless and thirdly to Sarah Law who had a large
family by him. Sarah Law McCance spent most of her life at Suffolk and after
her husband's death she lived at Glenville. All of her children who reached adult
life did well: the eldest, James, became an RM at Newry and lived most of his life
in England; Jane married John McCance Blizard, whose father had married a
Knocknagoney McCance – he was an MD of Liverpool University, and went to
practise in England; two of their sons were in business but also involved in the
linen industry and were well off – these were John Wellington Stouppe

McCance, Director of the Ulster Bank, and Henry Jones McCance who became Managing Director of the Ulster Bank; Mary married Colonel Archibald Campbell and Elizabeth Eleanor married George Callwell of Lismoyne; Charlotte Georgiana, youngest daughter, appears to have kept house for Henry Jones McCance at Larkfield.

The McCance Hunt Cup. Presented to John McCance, MP by his many hunting friends, *c* 1830.

MAGNI UM

WILLIAM·McCANCE'S
SUFFOLK-HEMP

William McCance, uncle of John McCance MP, died unmarried in 1810 leaving the bleach green at Suffolk and business at Kilwee to his nephew for life with reversion to John's eldest son William. There is plenty of evidence from various sources that when William McCance died in 1810 the family was wealthy and he himself appears to have been a rich man. He left money, the interest on a sum of £4,000 to each of his five nieces: Sarah and Rachel McCance, daughters of his late brother David; Rachel and Isabella Stouppe, daughters of his sister Mary McCance Stouppe; and Mary Stouppe, wife of John McCance Stouppe. Rachel and Isabella Stouppe resided with William McCance and kept house for him, so he bequeathed to them the 'New Carriage which he had lately purchased with the Black Mares which usually draw the same'. William McCance left Suffolk and land to his nephew John McCance of Roselands along with the residue of his estate to be divided with John McCance Stouppe of Glenville. Larkfield appears to have been built subsequent to William McCance's death in 1823/4 by Isabella Stouppe as a home for herself and her sister Rachel.

William McCance, son of John McCance MP, married Isabella Russell of Newforge in 1824, and settled first at Farmhill where their eldest son, John was born in 1825. However in the same year they moved to Glenville after the death of John McCance Stouppe and the marriage of his widow to Dr J.R. Park of Hampstead, for the next four children, Willie, Finlay, Kate and Holmes were born at Glenville. Prosperity continued until John McCance MP died in 1835 leaving the estate, consisting of The Glen, and land on the west side of it to which had been added at least 200 more acres. When William moved to Suffolk following his father's death he and his family were surrounded by the temptations of an enjoyable and relaxed life style: firstly he was the possessor of a large and valuable estate with a long wooded glen and water power in it; and secondly, Belfast included a number of wealthy families e.g. the Charleys, the Russells, the Holmes, the Joys, the Houstons, the Hunters etc. There was a good deal of mutual entertainment, small point-to-point horse racing and plenty of shooting and fishing within a reasonable level for the young folk. However the honeymoon period for the Irish linen bleachers was rapidly drawing to a close and the situation required enterprise

William McCance,
Suffolk House,
1801–1865
R.F. McCance

and adaptation.

William inherited the Suffolk works and linen business, but his father John had a large family to provide for and William got little beyond Suffolk which his father had been able to mortgage heavily. The Glenville property was left by John to his sons by his third marriage, John Wellington Stouppe McCance and Henry Jones McCance. They did not continue the bleach green at Glenville which they let to their elder half-brother William McCance of Suffolk and for some years he ran both the bleach greens, Glenville and Suffolk, with the warehouse, lapping rooms and residence at Suffolk. William must have been hoping to live as a merchant or a commission agent when he made his journeys to England and elsewhere and for this he would have required capital and hard work. In fact, William spent a lot of time away from home, sea bathing, fishing, shooting and enjoying himself. In 1857 William sold Suffolk to his much younger half brother J.W.S. McCance, gave up his tenancy of Glenville and retired from business, dying in 1865.

William had ten children two of whom died young, but his third son Finlay McCance (1829–1890) was very successful and retrieved the fortunes of his branch of the family. Finlay and his step-uncle Henry Jones McCance (1829–1900) had entered into partnership about 1850 as Linen Merchants and Commission Agents in Belfast. He was also, for a while, a director of the Ulster Spinning Company and a director of York Street Flax Spinning Company, and, while he had these businesses in Belfast, lived in No. 12 University Square. However when William, Finlay's father, died in 1865, Finlay returned to live at

Suffolk House. Some years earlier his step-uncle Henry had left their business partnership and had returned to help his brother, John Wellington Stouppe McCance, going into partnership with him to bleach linen at Glenville, but latterly they had had other business interests and in the late 1860s were anxious to sell Glenville and their part of the Suffolk estate. Finlay was persuaded to buy Glenville and that part of the estate from Henry by his uncle William Russell who promised to leave him £26,000 to settle the mortgage but eventually left a life interest in this to another person so despite the boom in the linen industry after the American Civil War Finlay was in trouble and had to turn the whole estate into a limited liability company. Before this, in 1866, his father-in-law, James Macauley of Crumlin came to help Finlay who leased Glenville House to him and the two went into partnership bleaching linen at Glenville until his death in 1871 when his son Robert succeeded him. Robert Macauley took into partnership George Kidd and in 1873 the firm built an entirely new bleaching works below Glenville where an old bleach works had existed. Subsequently in 1882, after the death of Robert Macauley, a limited company, the Suffolk Linen Company, was formed in which Finlay McCance became principal shareholder.

The business did not do well and when Finlay McCance died in 1890 his only son, John Stouppe Finlay McCance, who had become a barrister in Dublin, took over control of the Suffolk Linen Company. He lived in Woodbourne House which Finlay had also purchased when he bought back the Glenville part of the estate. In 1896 he resuscitated the old Kilwee bleachworks below Suffolk which prospered as the Kilwee Bleaching Co., Ltd, and after the First World War was under the management of his son Henry Bristow McCance. J.S.F. McCance died in 1926, and in 1932 the Suffolk Linen Company was wound up by Harry McCance and the premises let as a bacon factory. An offer was made for the Kilwee Bleaching Co. and he accepted it, thus bringing to an end the association of the district with the name McCance and the linen industry for almost two hundred years.

BLEACH-GREEN NEAR BELFAST.

TO BE LET, THE BLEACH-GREEN, &c., OF "SUFFOLK."

The Lands of Suffolk, containing, by a recent survey, upwards of 360 acres, are held direct by deed from the Commissioners of Encumbered Estates in Ireland, free from all rent, but subject to tithe.

The Bleach-Green is within three miles of Belfast, and half-a-mile of the Dunmurry Station, on the Ulster Railway.

There are two waterfalls, of twenty feet each, at present occupied, and there is, also, another, of about forty feet, on the lands that could be made available.

The supply of water is most abundant, and that of spring water is, probably, one of the best in Ulster.

The one-half of Collin Glen, so remarkable for its picturesque scenery, is on these lands, the plantations of which contain above sixty acres, principally hardwood of nearly fifty years' growth, in thriving condition, and are most valuable.

The Bleach-Green, with such quantity of land as may be required, will be Let separate, as agreed on, or the entire would be Sold, and a great part of the purchase-money, if desired, would be allowed to remain, on the security of the premises.

The Mansion-House of Suffolk is large and commodious; it contains two reception-rooms thirty feet by twenty feet, with large entrance hall, ten bed-rooms, besides dressing-rooms, servants' apartments, &c., and every accommodation requisite for a large family and establishment.

There are two enclosed Yards, a walled Garden, with Greenhouse, Vinery, &c., in full bearing.

There are some admirable Villa sites in the grounds; and to a capitalist, who wished to employ all the water-power on the lands, a more eligible investment could not be had.

For further particulars, apply to the Proprietor, WILLIAM M'CANCE, Esq., Suffolk, Belfast; or, HENRY RUSSELL, Solicitor, Arthur-Street, Belfast.
May 23, 1856.   1361

McCance Bleach Green and Suffolk House to be let by William McCance

Belfast Mercury 27 May 1856

MCCANCE FAMILY TREE

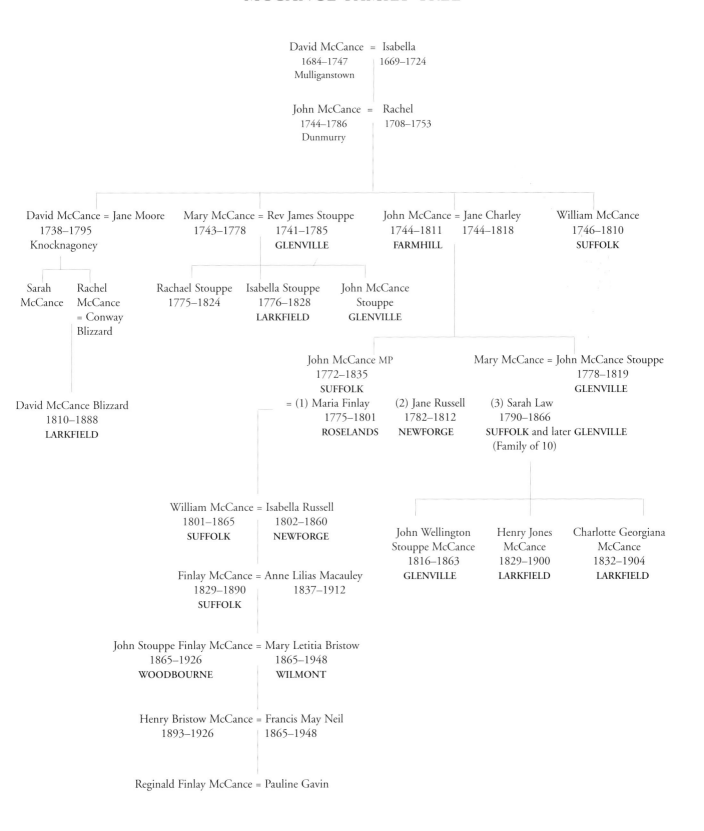

David McCance = Isabella
1684–1747 | 1669–1724
Mulliganstown

John McCance = Rachel
1744–1786 | 1708–1753
Dunmurry

David McCance = Jane Moore
1738–1795
Knocknagoney

Mary McCance = Rev James Stouppe
1743–1778 | 1741–1785
GLENVILLE

John McCance = Jane Charley
1744–1811 | 1744–1818
FARMHILL

William McCance
1746–1810
SUFFOLK

Sarah
McCance

Rachel
McCance
= Conway
Blizzard

Rachael Stouppe
1775–1824

Isabella Stouppe
1776–1828
LARKFIELD

John McCance
Stouppe
GLENVILLE

David McCance Blizzard
1810–1888
LARKFIELD

John McCance MP
1772–1835
SUFFOLK
= (1) Maria Finlay
1775–1801
ROSELANDS

Mary McCance = John McCance Stouppe
1778–1819
GLENVILLE

(2) Jane Russell
1782–1812
NEWFORGE

(3) Sarah Law
1790–1866
SUFFOLK and later **GLENVILLE**
(Family of 10)

John Wellington
Stouppe McCance
1816–1863
GLENVILLE

Henry Jones
McCance
1829–1900
LARKFIELD

Charlotte Georgiana
McCance
1832–1904
LARKFIELD

William McCance = Isabella Russell
1801–1865 | 1802–1860
SUFFOLK | **NEWFORGE**

Finlay McCance = Anne Lilias Macauley
1829–1890 | 1837–1912
SUFFOLK

John Stouppe Finlay McCance = Mary Letitia Bristow
1865–1926 | 1865–1948
WOODBOURNE | **WILMONT**

Henry Bristow McCance = Francis May Neil
1893–1926 | 1865–1948

Reginald Finlay McCance = Pauline Gavin

GLENVILLE HOUSE
SUFFOLK ROAD

Glenville House
Delacherois Estate

Rev. James Stouppe,
1741–1785
R.F. McCance

GLENVILLE was situated on the east side of Colin Glen and was one of the McCance family houses. Mention is first made of the house in the mid-18th century when Rev. James Stouppe (1741–1785) married Mary, daughter and second child of John McCance (1711–1786) of Dunmurry. The house stood between the Stewartstown Road and the large lake or dam which ornamented the grounds, the waters of which were fed by a lead from the Glen River and controlled by a sluice gate. The photograph is a reproduction from a watercolour painting showing Glenville House which has a Queen Anne style of architecture, a two-storey five-bay wide house with hipped roof and a rear wing. At the front there is a wide entrance through a columned porch. The painting shows Colin Mountain on the extreme right. The estate had three gate lodges and the grounds crossed the road at Suffolk Road, including the upper glen which was beautifully wooded and had deer. The glen is now all part of the recently established Colin Glen Trust who acquired the upper glen from the National Trust. Glenville Dam water was used in the Glenville bleaching and later by the Suffolk Linen Co., Ltd, which was near Glenville.

Rev. James Stouppe was a Presbyterian minister in Dunmurry who lived at Glenville and was in the linen trade. After his death in 1785 the house was occupied by his son John McCance Stouppe (1764–1819), who was only twenty-one when he married Mary McCance, the sister of his business partner, John McCance MP. The land at Glenville and the accompanying water power were used as a bleach green. The death of John McCance Stouppe freed Glenville because Mary McCance, his widow, soon married Dr Park, a doctor in Hampstead. William McCance (1801–1865), eldest son of John McCance MP, married Isabella Russell (1802–1860) and after living at Farmhill moved to Glenville in 1827. However, on the death of his father in 1835, the family moved to Suffolk in 1836 and John McCance's widow Sarah (Law) McCance (1790–1866) and family transferred to Glenville.

After Sarah McCance's death in 1866 Glenville was occupied for some thirty years by James Macaulay, who was father-in-law to Finlay McCance of Suffolk House. In 1888 Glenville was sold to Thomas Caffrey, owner of the mountain brewery on the Glen Road, which became the property of Bass Charrington (Ireland) Ltd. Glenville was unoccupied after 1901 and fell into disrepair.

Glenville dam taken in the early spring late 1930s
R.F. McCance

SUFFOLK HOUSE

Suffolk House, *c* 1900
PRONI

Suffolk House stood until 1980 in land adjacent to the housing development to which it gave its name, and faced south-east across the Lagan Valley with its back to Colin Mountain. The oldest part of the building dated from the late 18th century when William McCance (1746–1810), youngest son of John McCance (1711–1786) of Dunmurry, owned a bleach green there as well as using part of his house as lapping rooms for the linen. John McCance MP (1772–1835) moved into the house in 1811 after the death of his uncle William. In 1824 he rebuilt and considerably enlarged it by adding the main front block which had an impressive hipped roof. Dixon describes the front section as having a small portico with two columns, stepped quoins at each corner, and regular bays of windows, with a projecting band of stone dividing the storeys. Eileen Black states: 'The dining room, which was to the left of the porch, has a fine plaster work centrepiece in the ceiling, and large decorative medallions, cartouche-shaped, placed at regular intervals around the walls, at picture rail height.' The earlier house lay behind the Georgian building and at right angles to it, with walls of dark hand-dressed basalt stone almost three feet thick. Crowned chimney pots, which were used on the Georgian wing, were also found on the earlier building and were probably added *c* 1824, when John McCance was unifying both old and new wings. In April 1835 valuation records show that while the greater part of the entire house was nearly new the stables and coach house were older. Although William McCance had used the old building as his residence close to his bleach green, John McCance MP, after improving Suffolk House had all bleaching transferred to Glenville. In the middle of the 19th century Suffolk was a very pleasant area with the mountains and glens around Suffolk House, heavily wooded, and full of game.

A contemporary view of the McCance houses is given by Philip Dixon Hardy in his book *The Northern Tourist* published in 1830:

> The country in this direction (south west), onwards along the foot and side of the mountain presents a scene of the most pleasing and gratifying description – numerous extensive bleach greens with the houses and finely planted demesnes of the wealthy proprietors. The green of John Sinclair Esq. first presents itself and, a little further on, that of William McCance Esq. On the right hand side of the road stands the private residence of the latter gentleman, an elegant though plain building with handsome pleasure grounds … In ascending the hill to the left appears the magnificent mansion of John McCance Esq. of Suffolk – the most splendid, perhaps, belonging to any man of business in the kingdom.

John McCance, MP,
1772–1835
R.F. McCance

Suffolk House continued in McCance ownership until 1922 when Isabella Russell McCance (1861–1956), eldest daughter of Finlay of Suffolk (1829–1890) and Annie Lilias Macauley (1837–1912) left it, and the house was sold to Mr Gaffikin who occupied the property until 1926. Remaining vacant until 1937 it was bought by Mr G.A. Cameron and subsequently the large front rooms were used as a store by the Ministry of Food during World War II.

In 1945 the front part of the house was leased to an Austrian refugee and scientist, Otto Harriman, who established in it a small business, Ulster Pearls Ltd, making artificial pearls. The business was successful until around 1975 when the hall and front rooms were gutted by a fire thought to have been malicious. The older back section of Suffolk House was occupied by Mrs G.A. Cameron until around 1980 when it was destroyed on a demolition order to facilitate the widening of the Stewartstown Road.

LARKFIELD

LARKFIELD was situated on Black's Road, Dunmurry and appears to have been built around 1824, being one of the largest properties in the area. The house was of the late Georgian period and was two-storey five-bay with hipped and slated roof. The windows had plain sashes and single-storey bays projected at the sides of the building. A porch on the front elevation appears of more recent construction.

John McCance of Suffolk took a lease of forty-nine acres with a farm in 1823 from the Marquis of Donegall and in 1824 there is reference to a lease between John McCance and Isabella Stouppe, of Larkfield. She died in March 1828 leaving the house and farm at Larkfield to her cousin Sarah on trust for the use of the children or child of Sarah's sister Rachel Blizard née McCance. Sarah was empowered to sell or dispose of the said farm and house of Larkfield if she should think this fit and advantageous. Indeed Sarah McCance did put Larkfield up for auction in August 1828 when Henderson Black purchased it for £1,725 and lived there until 1843 when the property was bought by Samuel Vance on behalf of David Blizard, son of Rachel McCance and Conway Blizard. In the 1834 valuation Larkfield House was the largest in the townland being fifty-five feet in length, thirty-five feet wide and twenty-three feet high.

David Blizard (1810–1888) occupied Larkfield from 1843 to 1866 although he advertised the house for sale in the *Belfast News Letter* of 19 August 1865 asking a price of £4,100. Larkfield was described as roomy and cheerful having two

reception, seven bedrooms; two enclosed yards, with stabling, coach house and excellent gardens. However Larkfield remained in family ownership as a sale is recorded 20 December 1866 from David Blizard to Henry Jones McCance, who occupied it until his death in 1900. His sister Charlotte Georgiana also lived there, keeping house for him, and she lived on there till her death in 1904, leaving Larkfield to her nephew George Callwell (1850–1921) who had married Sarah Law Blizard (1850–1931).

After World War II Larkfield was used as a Ministry of Education training centre for teachers and then demolished to make way for a new intermediate secondary school.

A carriage at the doorway of Larkfield with possible occupants, Henry Jones McCance and his sister Charlotte Georgiana

Private Collection

Henry Jones McCance, DL, 1829–1900 (1896).

Artist: Theodore Blake Wirgman, 1848–1925

MAGNI UM

FARMHILL HOUSE

Farmhill

MBR

ARMHILL is situated on the west side of Black's Road, Dunmurry and is not visible from the road. The house is three-bay, two-storey and possibly designed by Lanyon or Turner. The roof is hipped and slated, walls are of red brick with stone dressings, windows have plain sashes and single-storey bays project at the sides of the building. A courtyard at the rear is flanked by two-storey stone buildings, one of which survives from pre-1830.

John McCance (1744–1811) of Farmhill, Dunmurry married in 1771 Jane Charley (1744–1818), daughter of John Charley of Finaghy. Their son, John McCance born 1772, eventually took over his uncle William's house at Suffolk and became MP for Belfast. This is the first mention of Farmhill where John McCance farmed while his brother William set up a bleach green at Ballycullo which is roughly where Suffolk House was first built with the bleaching works adjacent. Farmhill was one of the McCance family homes and William, son of John McCance, occupied Farmhill for a short period after his marriage to

Isabella Russell on 30 April 1824. Apart from family usage the house appears to have been let in the mid-1800s.

In 1869 Henry Jones McCance of Larkfield sold lands at Farmhill to William Coates, JP, of Glentoran, for the sum of £2,000. Edward Richardson (1845–1901), son of Jonathan Richardson of Lambeg House married Eleanor Coates, daughter of William Coates, in 1866. William Coates had the new Farmhill House built for his daughter Eleanor on the old McCance land in 1870 and left it to her and her husband on his death in 1878.

Farmhill
MBR

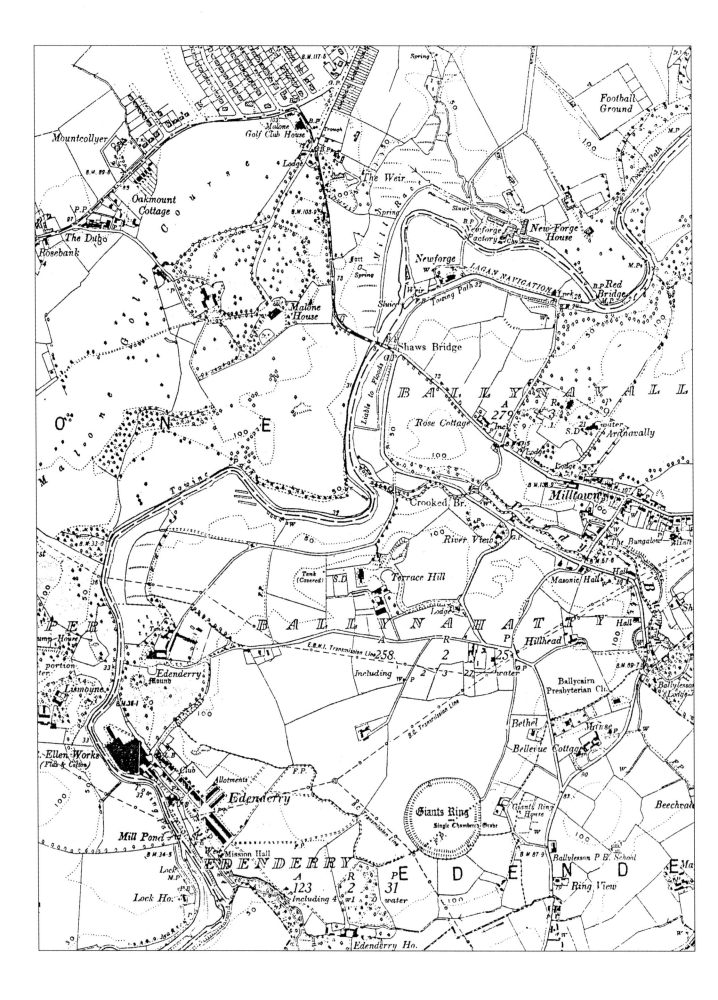

8

EDENDERRY

Barges at Edenderry

Romeo Toogood

Reproduced with the kind permission of the Trustees of the National Museums and Galleries of Northern Ireland

EDENDERRY HOUSE

Edenderry House, *c* 1890
Mrs F. Weir

E DENDERRY HOUSE was described in the *Ordnance Survey Memoirs* of 1833 for the Parish of Drumbo as the residence of H.W. Russell Esquire, the house being pleasantly situated near the River Lagan. In fact the house was situated not far from Shaw's Bridge on the County Down side of the river Lagan in a sheltered position and surrounded by trees. A late 18th century building Edenderry House was five bays wide, three storeys high with slated roof and four chimneys, two being at the gable ends. There was a central doorcase with Tuscan columns and horizontal glazing bars in side-lights and a deep undecorated fanlight. Internally the house is reputed to have had a notable staircase.

Records show that the Russell family was already established at Edenderry by the mid-17th century and early in the 18th century had established a bleach green. Belinda Jupp in her *Heritage Gardens Inventory* of 1992 records for Edenderry House, 'House of 1734 now gone. Fine stands of beech and lime along river and road. Planted motte. Walled garden.' In fact Lendrick's 1780 map of Co. Antrim shows a bleach green at Edenderry, on a site belonging to John Russell. The *Belfast News Letter* of 28 April 1758 reported a list of one hundred linen drapers who were boycotting hawkers selling brown linen cloth and this list included William Russell of Edenderry who would have been attending linen markets to buy brown linen for bleaching. In 1780 John Russell was appointed

Edenderry House, doorway
MBR

a member of the committee to negotiate with John Barclay about Williamson's lime process for bleaching and this shows that he was then recognised within the trade and must have been bleaching considerable quantities of linen.

It would seem reasonable to assume that it was during the latter half of the 18th century that the new Edenderry House was built on site close to the original Russell home. A map of Edenderry drawn for William Russell, Esq., and dated 1811 clearly shows a mill close to the river Lagan and another larger building nearby which is marked Bleach Mills. Edenderry House is marked and details are given of distances along the

William Russell's signature drawn on a linen map of Edenderry, 1811
PRONI

avenue from the house which crossed the Minnowburn and eventually joined the road leading to Shaw's Bridge. E.R.R. Green states that around 1830 the Russells gave up linen bleaching and turned the premises into a flour mill, the Valuation books describing two buildings, one which had been a bleach works and then was a flour mill and a second building which had been converted from a beetling mill to a flour mill.

In 1855 William Liddell and John Shaw Brown set up in the linen business in Donaghcloney supplying yarn to weavers and collecting the cloth which they then bleached at Banoge bleachgreen. However in the early 1860s they terminated their agreement and at this point John Shaw Brown purchased the old mill and bleachyard at Edenderry, Shaw's Bridge, Belfast, setting up a large and well equipped power loom weaving factory named the 'St Ellen Works', in honour of his wife who was called Ellen. John S. Brown & Sons, Ltd, became a well known

Edenderry House, *c* 1960
P.J. Rankin

George Herbert Brown, JP,
1855–1908, son of the late John
Shaw Brown, JP

firm in the production of linen damask and very fine linen handkerchiefs and
tablecloths which were sold world wide. The company worked under contract
for the supply of linen damask to such companies as the old railways, LNER and
LMS.

John S. Brown & Sons developed the village at Edenderry, building around
ninety houses, and a further thirty houses at Purdysburn, for workers about
1900. There was a plant in the factory to produce coal gas and this was supplied to the houses for domestic use although bathrooms were not installed,
and workers could book the use of a bath in the factory where a number were
available. Edenderry village also had a shop dedicated to supplying the employees and orders might be left in the morning for collection after work. The company had their main warehouse at 12 Bedford Street, Belfast, which was bombed
and totally destroyed in 1972. Unfortunately the factory had to close down in
the late 1970s due to the lack of demand for linen products.

John Shaw Brown (1822–1887) lived in Edenderry House until his death in
1887 and it was owned by the Brown family until the mid-twentieth century.
Eventually the house was demolished in 1976.

Edenderry Village. Houses built
by John Shaw Brown and Sons
for workers in their factory

JFR

THE RUSSELLS OF EDENDERRY AND NEWFORGE

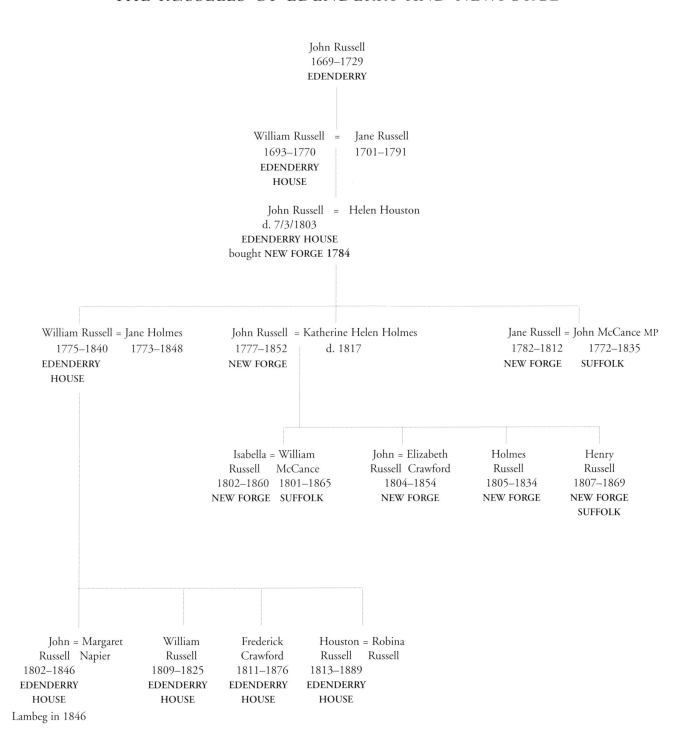

John Russell
1669–1729
EDENDERRY

William Russell = Jane Russell
1693–1770   1701–1791
**EDENDERRY
HOUSE**

John Russell = Helen Houston
d. 7/3/1803
EDENDERRY HOUSE
bought **NEW FORGE 1784**

William Russell = Jane Holmes
1775–1840   1773–1848
**EDENDERRY
HOUSE**

John Russell = Katherine Helen Holmes
1777–1852   d. 1817
NEW FORGE

Jane Russell = John McCance MP
1782–1812   1772–1835
NEW FORGE   **SUFFOLK**

Isabella = William
Russell   McCance
1802–1860 1801–1865
NEW FORGE **SUFFOLK**

John = Elizabeth
Russell Crawford
1804–1854
NEW FORGE

Holmes
Russell
1805–1834
NEW FORGE

Henry
Russell
1807–1869
**NEW FORGE
SUFFOLK**

John = Margaret
Russell Napier
1802–1846
**EDENDERRY
HOUSE**
Lambeg in 1846

William
Russell
1809–1825
**EDENDERRY
HOUSE**

Frederick
Crawford
1811–1876
**EDENDERRY
HOUSE**

Houston = Robina
Russell   Russell
1813–1889
**EDENDERRY
HOUSE**

JOHN SHAW BROWN

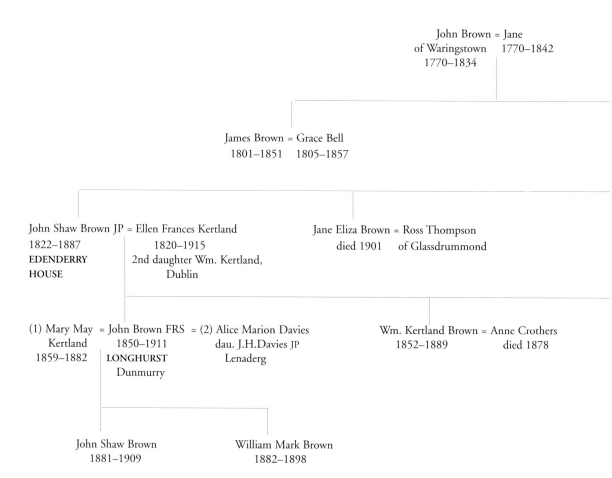

John Brown = Jane
of Waringstown   1770–1842
1770–1834

James Brown = Grace Bell
1801–1851   1805–1857

John Shaw Brown JP = Ellen Frances Kertland
1822–1887   1820–1915
EDENDERRY   2nd daughter Wm. Kertland,
HOUSE   Dublin

Jane Eliza Brown = Ross Thompson
died 1901   of Glassdrummond

(1) Mary May   = John Brown FRS   = (2) Alice Marion Davies
Kertland   1850–1911   dau. J.H.Davies JP
1859–1882   **LONGHURST**   Lenaderg
                          Dunmurry

Wm. Kertland Brown = Anne Crothers
1852–1889   died 1878

John Shaw Brown
1881–1909

William Mark Brown
1882–1898

OF EDENDERRY

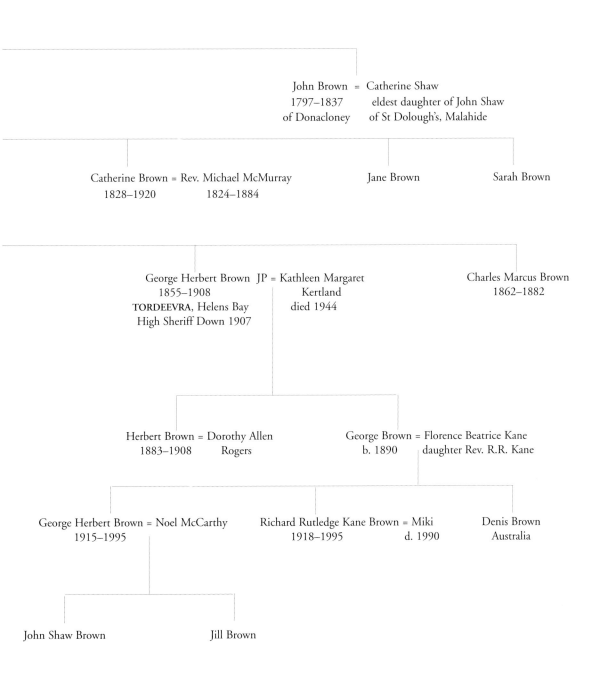

John Brown = Catherine Shaw
1797–1837   eldest daughter of John Shaw
of Donacloney   of St Dolough's, Malahide

Catherine Brown = Rev. Michael McMurray   Jane Brown   Sarah Brown
1828–1920   1824–1884

George Herbert Brown JP = Kathleen Margaret   Charles Marcus Brown
1855–1908   Kertland   1862–1882
TORDEEVRA, Helens Bay   died 1944
High Sheriff Down 1907

Herbert Brown = Dorothy Allen   George Brown = Florence Beatrice Kane
1883–1908   Rogers   b. 1890   daughter Rev. R.R. Kane

George Herbert Brown = Noel McCarthy   Richard Rutledge Kane Brown = Miki   Denis Brown
1915–1995   1918–1995   d. 1990   Australia

John Shaw Brown   Jill Brown

NEWFORGE

Newforge House. Drawn by
Joseph Molloy, Belfast, and
engraved by E.K. Proctor,
London, 1832.

Linen Hall Library

AN ENCHANTING PICTURE of Newforge was drawn by Joseph Molloy, engraved by E.K. Proctor, and published in *Belfast Scenery in Thirty Views* in 1832. Newforge was an elegant mid-Georgian house set in a maturely planted landscape and faced south eastwards to the river Lagan. The large four-square, two-storey house was five bays wide with slated hipped roof, having a full raised basement and an elaborate, pedimented doorway approached up a splayed flight of steps. The house stood towards the end of Newforge Lane until it was demolished in the 1960s to allow for industrial development.

Originally Newforge was the site of an iron works established around 1630 and reference has been made to it as early as 1641 when a Captain Lawson, who was active in trying to quell the Irish Rebellion of 1641 in Belfast and Lisburn, described the iron-works as two miles from Belfast on the river Lagan. The rebellion of 1641 greatly injured the iron works business and it disappeared entirely with the extinction of the Irish woods. However, by the mid-18th century a bleach green had been established and in 1784 John Russell of Edenderry bought the bleach green at Newforge. It was possibly he who built the new

Newforge House and the main doorway, *c* 1960

P.J. Rankin

house *c* 1790 at Newforge for his second son John, who married in 1801 Katherine Helen, daughter of John Holmes, a Belfast banker. His brother William, who had already married Jennet Holmes, a sister of Katherine Helen, inherited Edenderry House and the bleach green on his father's death in 1803.

Meanwhile Jane Russell, youngest daughter of John Russell of Edenderry and sister of William and John, married John McCance MP, after the death of his first wife Maria in 1801. Jane had no children and died in 1812. However, there was to be yet another link between the Russell and McCance families in that William McCance, eldest son of John McCance MP, married Isabella Russell, daughter of John Russell of Newforge and Katherine Holmes, on 30th April 1824. Their eldest son John McCance (1825–1869), kept a diary, which is still in the possession of the McCance family, giving a record from 1827 to 1856 of the social life of the McCances and their friends. From this diary one can paint a picture of the period which included dinners at Newforge, balls at Suffolk, shooting parties in Counties Down and Antrim and the families of the McCances, Russells, Holmes, Hunters and Charleys who socialised together.

In 1800 Thomas Ferguson, who had previously owned a bleach green at Craigarogan near Dunadry, acquired from the Russells of Edenderry the old-established bleachworks at Newforge, although John Russell continued to live in the house at Newforge until his death on 23rd November 1852. Indeed, the Russells were still at Newforge in 1854 when John McCance recorded in his diary for April 7th:

> Holmes and I went to Newforge to a Party this was the first party there (that we were at) since Grandpappas death and the first time I ever was at a dance in that house.

Unfortunately John Russell (son of the above John Russell) died on 6th November 1854 and this effectively brought to an end their occupancy of Newforge.

Thomas Ferguson had for a time partners in his firm, firstly John Russell who had also a bleachworks at Deramore, on the County Down side of the river Lagan, and secondly Lawson Annesley (d. 1838). Thomas Ferguson died in 1833, and in Ballylesson Churchyard may be seen close together stones commemorative of the three families. At Newforge the bleachyard continued under the name of James Ferguson & Sons until 1880, when it finally appears to have closed. James Ferguson died in 1875 and is recorded as having lived at Newforge.

John Russell of Newforge House, 1777–1852

NMGNI UM

TERRACE HILL

Terrace hill, Ballynahatty Road, Edenderry is situated in the Lagan Valley Regional Park, approximately three miles south of Belfast city centre. The property occupies a height overlooking Shaw's Bridge, the river Lagan and Barnett's Park, close to Edenderry Village and the Giant's Ring.

The original Terrace Hill was built about 1856 by Frederick Russell (1811–1876), son of William Russell and Jane Holmes of Edenderry House. The house is recorded in the 1861 valuation for the townland of Ballynahatty and described as a roomy elegant new house built five years ago commanding a splendid view of the valley of the Lagan, well finished with projecting bow windows and having servants' rooms. Frederick Russell died in 1876 and the property passed successively through the Fergusons to W. Matthew and Isabella Coates who were living at Terrace Hill in 1898.

Edward A. Robinson (who was known as Ned) bought Terrace Hill in the early years of the 20th century. He is recorded as a churchwarden in the local parish church in 1909. However, after the Robinsons were bought out of Robinson & Cleaver in the 1930s, he had the house demolished, employing architects Young & McKenzie to build in 1936 a new house, again named Terrace Hill. The property has recently been described as a luxury dwelling house comprising a two-storey building of approximately 9,200 square feet, together with various out-buildings. The grounds include lawns, gardens and a swimming pool, and most of the surrounding land is owned by the National Trust and maintained as woodland and agricultural land.

Ned Robinson and his brother Harold were directors in the firm of Robinson & Cleaver Ltd, linen manufacturers, with retail premises in Regent Street, London, Liverpool and Belfast and a weaving factory, William Walker & Company, Banbridge. Their father Edward Robinson, JP, with John Cleaver founded Robinson & Cleaver, of Belfast, which was afterwards converted into a limited company, and of which Edward Robinson was Chairman until 1905. Robinson & Cleaver was first set up in 1884 as the Royal Belfast Linen Warehouse with premises newly built in Donegall Place. At the start, the business was principally mail order with a small retail section but over time this changed to a purely retail business. Robinson & Cleaver was floated as a company on the Stock Exchange in 1936 and at this time the Robinson family were bought out by De Steen & Company, who were merchant bankers. Ned Robinson occupied Terrace Hill until his death on 8th December 1947 aged 69.

Latterly, Terrace Hill was occupied by the Clokeys, followed by the Simms, and then the building was in use as a residential children's home for approximately twenty years until 1997, when the house was sold, again passing into private ownership.

Terrace Hill 1998
JFR

THE WEIR

The Weir

JFR

THE WEIR, 276 Malone Road, Belfast is situated on a hill overlooking the river Lagan at Shaw's Bridge, having views over the surrounding countryside. This is a very large 'Old English' style house in grey roughcast with stone chimneys and crenellated porch with Tudor-arched door, which was designed in 1916 by Blackwood & Jury, for Thomas Somerset, linen merchant. The house has small leaded panes and stone mullioned windows throughout, except for one large plate glass window to the drawing room, overlooking Shaw's Bridge, which is an original feature. Stables adjoining the garage were added in 1920.

Thomas Somerset was born and educated in Lisburn. After an initial training in the linen industry he built a considerable weaving factory in Hardcastle Street, Belfast, which specialised in plain goods such as sheets, pillowcases etc. which were often made in cotton. Somersets built up a considerable export business to the T. Eaton Company in Canada but also traded with Maceys, New York and Harrods, London. In the early years the company produced fine linen handkerchiefs, and linen sheets and pillowcases, which often had monograms embroidered to order. Thomas Somerset & Co., Ltd closed in 1971 and the factory was sold to a building developer.

Sir Thomas Somerset was MP for North Belfast between 1924 and 1945 and was knighted in 1944 for political services. He married in 1906, his wife coming from Baggeley House in Cheshire, and they had a son and daughter. The Somerset family often had guests to stay at The Weir, particularly from Canada, since they did a lot of business with the Eatons. The house was staffed by a cook, parlour maid and a gardener. Sir Thomas Somerset died in 1945 and The Weir was sold in 1972, after the death of Lady Somerset, remaining in private ownership.

Sir Thomas Somerset, MP
LL

Opposite:
Lissue House
DR JOHN PRESS

SELECT BIBLIOGRAPHY

An Archaeological Survey of County Down, edited by E.M. Jope, Belfast, 1966

ARMSTRONG, D.L., *The Growth of Industry in Northern Ireland,* Oxford, 1999

ATKINSON, A., *Ireland Exhibited to England in a Political and Moral Survey of her Population,* 2 vols., London, 1823

ATKINSON, EDWARD DUPRÉ, *History of Donaghcloney,* Dublin, 1898

BARR, W.N.C., *Derriaghy, A Short History of the Parish,* Belfast, 1974

BASSETT, G.H., *The Book of Antrim: A Manual and Directory,* Dublin, 1888

BASSETT, G.H., *County Down, 100 Years Ago,* Belfast, 1988, reprint of original, 1886

BEAUMONT, P. & MAGENNIS, H., *Princess Gardens School, A Goodly Heritage,* Belfast, 1993

BECKETT, J.C., et al, *Belfast, the Making of a City,* Belfast, 1983

Belfast Municipal Museum & Art Gallery, 'Coulsons of Lisburn', *Quarterly Notes* No. LVII, 1938

BELL, STANLEY, *Hart of Lisburn, Northern Ireland,* Lisburn, 1983

BENCE JONES, MARK, *A Guide to Irish Country Houses,* London, 1988

BENN, GEORGE, *History of Belfast,* London, 1877

BLACK, EILEEN, 'Suffolk House', *Lisburn Historical Society Journal,* vol. 2, 1979
'Wilmont, Dunmurry: a profile', ibid., vol. 4, 1982
'Ballydrain, Dunmurry – an estate through the ages', ibid., vol., 5, 1984
'A Glimpse of Drumbeg, 1750–1800', ibid., vol. 7, 1989

BLACKWOOD, R.W.T.H., *MS, Genealogies,* in Linen Hall Library, Belfast

BLAIR, MAY, *Once Upon the Lagan: The Story of the Lagan Canal,* Belfast, 1981

BRETT, C.E.B., *Buildings of County Antrim,* Belfast, 1996

BRETT, C.E.B., *Buildings of North Down,* Belfast, 2002

BRYSON, G. HERBERT, *Memories of a Long Life,* East Huntley, Dunmurry, 1982, privately printed

CARTER, WILLIAM, *A Short History of the Linen Trade,* Vol. ii, Belfast, 1952

CHARLEY, W.R.H., 'Charley Houses in Dunmurry', *Lisburn Historical Society Journal,* vol. 9, 1995

CLENDINNING, KIERAN, *A General Study of Waringstown,* Lurgan, 1970

COX, R.R., *The Parish of Kilbride,* Doagh, 1959

CRAWFORD, W.H., *The Hand Loom Weavers and the Ulster Linen Industry,* Belfast 1994

CRAWFORD, W.H., 'Lisburn at the coming of the Huguenots' and 'The Huguenots and the linen industry' in *The Huguenots and Ulster 1685–1985,* Lisburn, 1985

CRAWFORD, W.H., 'Ulster Landowners and the Linen Industry', in J.T. Ward and R.G. Wilson, eds, *Land and Industry: the Landed Estate and the Industrial Revolution,* 1971

CUMMINGS, MARY, *Letters Home to Lisburn, from America 1811–1815,* edited by Jimmy Irvine, Co. Antrim, 1982

DAY, ANGELIQUE & McWILLIAMS, PATRICK (eds), *Ordnance Survey Memoirs of Ireland,*
vol. 7, *Parishes of County Down II 1832–4, 1837,* Belfast, 1991
vol. 8, *Parishes of County Antrim II 1832–8,* Belfast, 1991
vol. 12, *Parishes of County Down III 1833–8,* Belfast, 1992

DEAN, J.A.K., *The Gate Lodges of Ulster, A Gazeteer,* UAHS, Belfast, 1994

DE BURGH, LYDIA, *Another Way of Life,* Coolatin Press, Clough, Downpatrick, 1999

DIXON, HUGH, 'Honouring Thomas Jackson (1807–1890) (architect)', *Proceedings and Reports of the Belfast Natural History and Philosophical Society,* Sessions 1970/71–1976/77, second series, vol. 9

GILL, CONRAD, *The Rise of the Irish Linen Industry,* Oxford, 1923

GILLESPIE, R.G., *Settlement and Survival on an Ulster Estate, The Brownlow Leasebook, 1667–1711,* PRONI, Belfast, 1988

GREEN, E.R.R., *The Industrial Archaeology of Co. Down,* Belfast, 1963

GREEN, E.R.R., *The Lagan Valley 1800–1850,* London, 1949

GREEN, W.J., *A Concise History of Lisburn and neighbourhood,* Belfast, 1906

HADDOCK, JOSIAH, *A Parish Miscellany, A Review of Donaghcloney Parish from earliest times to the present day,* Lurgan Mail Press, 1949

HARDY, PHILIP DIXON, *The Northern Tourist,* 1830

HORNER, J., *The Linen Trade of Europe During the Spinning Wheel Period,* Belfast, 1920

JOHNSTON, JOHN MOORE, *Heterogenea or Medley,* Downpatrick, 1803

LAWLOR, H.C., 'The Genesis of the Linen Thread Trade', *Ulster Journal of Archaeology,* series 3, Vol. VI, 1943

LAWLOR, H.C., 'Rise of the Linen Merchants in the Eighteenth Century', *Irish and International Fibres and Fabrics Journal,* 1941–1943

LARMOUR, PAUL, *The Architectural Heritage of Malone and Stranmillis,* Belfast, 1991

LARMOUR, PAUL, *Belfast, An Illustrated Architectural Guide,* Belfast, 1987

LEWIS, ELIZABETH, 'An 18th-century Linen Damask Tablecloth from Ireland', in *Textile History,* Vol 15 (2), 1984

LEWIS, SAMUEL, *Topographical Dictionary of Ireland,* Dublin, 1837

LONGFIELD, ADA K. (Mrs H.G. Leask), 'Old Wallpapers in Ireland', *Irish Georgian Society,* Vol. X, No.1, January–March 1967.

McCALL, HUGH, *Ireland and her Staple Manufactures,* second edition, Belfast, 1865

McCANCE, JOHN, *Journal (1825–1869),* PRONI, Belfast

McCLENAGHAN, C., *Thomas Jackson,* 1993, research report in Queen's University Belfast Library

McCUTCHEON, W.A., *The Industrial Archaeology of Northern Ireland,* Belfast, 1980

MACKEY, BRIAN, *Lisburn, The Town and Its People, 1873–1973,* Belfast, 2000

MACKEY, BRIAN J., 'Centres of Drawloom Damask Linen Weaving in Ireland in the 18th and 19th Centuries', *Riggisberger Berichte,* Vol 7, 1999

MARSHALL, H.C., *The Parish of Lambeg,* Lisburn, 1933

NEILL, M., *Recollections of The Parish of Drumbeg, Diocese of Down,* Belfast, 1996

Northern Ireland Heritage Gardens Committee, *Heritage Gardens Inventory 1992,* Compiled by Belinda Jupp, Institute of Irish Studies, The Queen's University of Belfast

PIERCE, RICHARD & COEY, ALASTAIR, *Taken for Granted,* Belfast, 1984

PROCTOR, E.K., *Belfast Scenery in Thirty Views 1832.* With a modern commentary by Fred Heatley and Hugh Dixon, Belfast, 1983

RANKIN, J.F., *The Heritage of Drumbo,* Belfast, 1982

RICHARDSON, JAMES N., *The Quakri at Lurgan and Grange,* Bessbrook, 1899

RICHARDSON, JAMES N., *Reminiscences of 'Friends' in Ulster,* Gloucester [1911]

RUTHERFORD, GEORGE, *Old families of Carrickfergus and Ballynure,* Belfast, 1995

SCOTT, ROBERT, *A Breath of Fresh Air: The Story of Belfast's Parks,* Belfast, 2000

STEVENSON, J., *Two Centuries of Life in Down 1600-1800,* Belfast, 1920

TOTTEN, JEAN, *Gleanings from Glenavy Parish,* Newcastle, 1980

WAKEFIELD, EDWARD, *An Account of Ireland, Statistical and Political,* London, 1812

WILLIAMS, JEREMY, *A Companion Guide to Architecture in Ireland 1837–1921,* Dublin, 1994

WILSON, ALEC, *Fragments that remain,* Sussex, 1950

YOUNG, A., *Tour in Ireland 1776–1779,* ed. A.W. Hutton, London, 1892

YOUNG, R.M., *Belfast and the Province of Ulster in the twentieth century,* Belfast, 1909

INDEX